The Best

of

Both Worlds

A. L. Watkines

The Best of Both Worlds
Copyright © 2013 A. L. Watkines

All rights reserved. Except for use in any review, the reproduction or utilization of this work in whole or in part in any form by any electronic, mechanical or other means, now known or hereafter invented, including xerography, photocopying and recording, or in any information storage or retrieval system, is forbidden without the written permission of the author, A. L. Watkines. He can be reached at: mralwatkines@yahoo.com.

ISBN - 10:1494354853
ISBN - 13: 978-1494354855

Authored by A. L. Watkines
Edited by C. Sanders
Cover by KRose Designs

DEDICATION

This book is dedicated to those who showed me how beautiful I am and to those that remind me constantly what a great gift God has placed upon me. To those who taught me the Christen way when I refused to believe there was a way. To those who listened when I spoke the words God told me to speak.

I am dedicating this book to my three daughters - LaKeysha, Keysha and Maxine, who showed me what love is in the purest form. Lastly, I dedicate this book to my late wife, Arlene LaKeysha Watkines, who died of breast cancer in 1992.

A. L. WATKINES

BOOK OF LOVE

If I could write a book of love it would be a best seller in the book stores.

For my first chapter I would tell the different ways I have found to love you. In this chapter, I would share with the world about the day I first met you; the first time I talked with you and the first time I heard your voice and felt you spirit move within me and the beauty that I saw on the inside of you. I would tell them of how you have me trusting not only your love but God's love.

The second chapter I would tell them of the seed that your father planted within your mother in order for God to create you to be the woman that He would have you to be and not the woman that the world would see you to be. The joy that he has placed within you, I would tell them of how you have given me a new outlook on love and what it takes to love.

Now in my third chapter I would share with them your past hurt and pain. Telling them of my promise to never let it happen again, I would tell how God has seen you through and how I will walk beside you and not in front of you. I would tell them of your eyes that let me see into your soul.

In my fourth chapter, I would share with them of the love that you have to share, that make you better then any other woman that has been in my past I would tell them of your passion that consist of a nature high and of your willingness to love inspired of your past mistakes. I would tell them of the gift that God has instilled within you; of your warmth and understanding for love, and how you have taken the breath out of me and made me weak in both my knees. I would tell them of the passion you have instilled within me and yet I have touched you with my hands but most of all I would tell them of the joy you have given to me. Yet from the worlds point of view you don't even know me, I would tell of your special touch as a Black woman and of you heritage as a Black African queen. I would tell them of your lips that is made of fruit from the best of fruit trees and your hips that move like the waves of an ocean sea. I would tell of your body that could bring any nation to it knees and make a blind man beg God for eye's to see.

In my fifth chapter I would tell of your hopes and dreams and what it would take for me to make them a reality. I would tell of how God has joined you and me to teach you how to love me and me you; for what God has join together let no man or woman take it under.

THE BEST OF BOTH WORLDS

CONTENTS

DEDICATION   3
         Book of Love   4

YOUTHFUL FOOLISHNESS
         Here in the Ghetto   9
         A Different Kind
          of Brotherly Love   10
         I Will Always Remember   11
         I Asked Him   12
         Just Another Black Man   14
         Mama's Love For Me   16
         Mr. Applesauces' Lounge   18
         What Has Come Over Me   20
         Last Night   21
         My Strong Black Sisters   23
         Never Liked Thick Women   25
         People Always Ask Me!   26
         Sometimes   28
         The Color of Chocolate Milk   29
         Went to the River   30
         Today I Felt A Tear   31
         Prime Beef   33
         That Night   35
         Sister I Promise   36
         My Special
          Nubian Queen   37
         Court of the Most High   40
         Are You Hungry?   41

BLINDED BY DARKNESS
         A Thief In the Night   44
         Hole In the Wall   45
         I Heard Them Making Love   47
         Men of Color   49
         She Was Ghetto   50
         Have You Ever Witnessed?   51
         Slim and Petite   52
         Turned On the
         Radio This Morning   53
         They Called Him Viper   54
         Somebody Hit Me   56
         Her Dirty Little Secret   57
         I Give You Me   58
         I Didn't Ask   59
         One Wish   60

A. L. WATKINES

CONTENTS

Just a 'Thank You'	62
Old School Brother	64
My Daddy	66
No Great Lover	67
A Tower of Gray	69

TOUCH OF FORBIDDEN LOVE

The Food Store of Love	72
My Nubian Queen	74
This Woman I Meet	76
Late Hours in the Night	77
It's So Easy To Love You	78
How Could God Make Her?	80
Loving and Being In Love	81
Made In His Image	83
A Raindrop	85
A Teardrop Of Love For You	86
Comfort of a Woman	88
A Touch of Unseen Beauty	90
Definition of a Real Man	91
A Black Man's Love	92
Starting My Day With You	94
Romeo & Juliet	95
You Got Me All Wrong	96
One Step Closer	97
Just a Little Bit of Love	99

REBIRTH

Manifestation of God	102
His Coming	104
I Made It Through	105
I Touched the Face of God Today	106
It's Not Too Late	108
Grant Me	109
A Battle For the Lord	111
My Prayer for You	112
One of God's Chosen Men	114
Precious Lord	115
Come As You Are	117
Today I Give You Peace	118
In the Lord's Presence	119

ACKNOWLEDGMENT   120

> # YOUTHFUL
> # FOOLISHNESS

HERE IN THE GHETTO

Here in the ghetto not everyone sale weed or drugs not everyone is poor or in need. See here in the ghetto we have some who have college and high school degrees. Look there's doctors and lawyers living here along with others that can grow up to be whatever they wish to be.

Here in the ghetto not every young lady or young man is a thief or a thug or a woman selling her body on the corner street. And not every young lady has a house full of babies waiting on food stamps to make their life complete. See here in the ghetto you can't always find a woman working to be all she can be.

Because here in the ghetto we have a different kind of love unfortunately there's no togetherness among us unless there's free food and drinks. Yes here in the ghetto it's true not every young child can write or read nor has the desire to play basketball or football as a way to have their dreams come true.

Here in the ghetto there is a special kind of music that is made which comes from the heart and soul - there's love songs, gospel and jazz.

Here in the ghetto new laws and careers are made. Many books have been written and read. See here in the ghetto you can always find a great cook. And many TV stars have been found here in the ghetto by how good they look.

Here in the ghetto many game shows have been won and yet there has been many race wars fought after the closing of the sun.

Here in the ghetto many mysteries have been found and there's very few fruit trees planted on good ground.

THE BEST OF BOTH WORLDS

HERE IN THE GHETTO

Here in the ghetto there have been many cars stolen and you can always find a shady tree mechanic getting paid. Here in the ghetto many love poems has been written and told while making love in bed. And here in the ghetto a beautician without a license gets ahead and believe it or not many beautiful hair styles have been made.

Here in the ghetto you can find car tires used as swings while family members and friends' playing card under the old oak tree. You might even find a block party.

Here in the ghetto you might find a boxer with hopes and dreams. Young girls believing they might be the next Ms. Black beauty queen.

Here in the ghetto the older folks remind us how life used to be and now we are able to say the words 'we are free'. You might even see a young lady in her tight shorts or blue jeans and she might be only eleven or thirteen.

Here in the ghetto you can find a young child that don't want to miss going to school. Babies running around without any shoes and old men standing on the corner trying to look cool. You might even find a long line at the city swimming pool. Here in the ghetto the police are always around.

And every blue moon you might hear a shout or a scream from around about. But just like people in the city; the people in the ghetto have the same kind of hopes and dreams.

A. L. WATKINES

A DIFFERENT KIND OF BROTHERLY LOVE

I remember when we used to climb grandmother's old oak tree. I was the oldest and he was younger then me. We used to walk through the river water with nothing on our feet and we would steal apples from the old lady tree across the street.

I recall when we barely had enough food to eat and the old wooden bunk beds where him and I used to sleep. Now I recall the times when my mother would pray at night for me. My how her words seem to touch something inside of me.

I recall the promise we made to always be there for each other when in need. I was six and he was three. Now looking back I am sure my fathers' seed did not fall far from the tree. See back then, I thought I was raising him but as I look back it seemed as if he was raising me.

Some would have called it brotherly love but I just called it me loving him and him loving me. Now that I have completed high school and he went on to get a college degree. I called myself a player. He got married and seemed as happy as could be.

Now there seemed like there were times when God was blessing him and my prayers were going unanswered and unseen. He had two sons and I had three girls and I knew his sons would carry out our family seed. So now each night I can't help but to thank God for blessing me with a brother who loved me.

I WILL ALWAYS REMEMBER

For it seemed as if I can't get you off of my mind or out of my head. Most of all out of my system although when I think of thoughts of you. I try to run away from them because they make me feel so good and unreal.

For you have given me so much of yourself, so much of your love for it is one of a kind.

Yet, I can't get over of the way that you make me feel inside even my daily thoughts are about you and the only one I have to blame is myself.

See I thought that I had you fooled didn't want to show you my hand and how much you meant to me but I should have never doubted you were from God you had to have been to get through to me and I must admit that all this time you were blowing my mind to the point I didn't want anybody else sometimes I seem to let my imagination get the best of me see things as they.

To the point I can't get you out of my heart, my soul or my emotions you're such a natural woman that I could love you in a hundred different ways with none of them seems to be the same

See I thank God for the respect you have for yourself and others and how you always remember where you come from and what God has brought you through in you I can see that God is real because I will always remember God's greatest gift to make a woman like you.

A. L. WATKINES

I ASKED HIM

I asked the Lord to make me a bit wiser because unlike when I was younger, I have now gotten older and what was once wisdom has begin to slip away from me.

I asked the Lord if He would entrusted within me knowledge and make me a bit kinder to those people around me and even more when it seem as if my enemies are more stronger than me.

See I asked the lord to make me a little bit manlier, because at time's it is hard for me to take defeated, because this devil has come again and this time she is wearing tight blue jeans.

So I asked the Lord to make me just a little bit finer see since I have gotten older, my head has become bold and I got corns on my feet and the women Lord don't even look at me.

Then I found myself asking Him to make me smile just a little bit more maybe give me some more teeth. Lord I was once a big whinier see I wanted everything my way and that is how it had to be.

So again I found myself asking Him to make me just a little quicker on my feet but most of all give me the strength to help another who's struggling and to think more of them and less of me. For this is my prayer, Lord, please make me a regular man.

I asked Him to make me just a little bit better at what He would have me to be and make me not so always ready to censure and blame others for what's going on with or around me.

Then I found myself asking Him to help me to be not so quite to see those who are doing better then me fall but please just a little bit more mature in my walk. Make me more giving and less of a taker but Lord please make me a regular man because perfect I will never be. I was born in sin from the crown of my head to the toes that is upon my feet.

I ASKED HIM

Then one day I found myself asking Him to create a new heart within me because at times this one I have seem to be missing a beat. I asked Him to please renew in me the man that everyone else sees within me and to take these splinters out of my eyes so that with His eyes I might be able to see. Lord I am asking you to **make a regular man out of me…...**

A. L. WATKINES

JUST ANOTHER BLACK MAN

How can I expect you to understand in your eyes I am a nobody? I am just another Black man living under the stars at night with no home or land.

Now I have no fancy clothes and no money in my hands. I have spent most of my life living on my own for I have no family or friends. See all my love ones have passed on and I live in a bad neighborhood in a boarded up home on someone else land. There is a drug dealer living next to me and the police will not take a stand; there is vacant land on the other side of me and I must admit at times I am afraid because I live here alone. Understand I am just another Black man.

But how can I expect you to understand for in your eyes I am a nobody just another Black man. Is it not true that God created me and called me Man? Is it not true He gave to me dominion over the Earth and the Sea and over the Land? Yes I have a hole in my shirt and dirt on my pants; my hair is nappy and there are scars on both my hands. Now my face might be wrinkled and my eyes might be summer red and my breath might be strong from the glass of white gin last night that I had.

Sure I carry a bible in my hand but how can I expect you to understand. For in your eyes I am a nobody just another black man. Trying to tell everybody that God time is at hand. Why do you judge me? It can not be because of the race that I am. For do you not believe that some day I will meet you in the Promise Land? But for now I am just another Black man and I don't expect you to understand.

See I've had my share of problems and I have faced death as a man. So now I am trying to share with others what God has given me as a man.

JUST ANOTHER BLACK MAN

At times I had no food to eat so I've taken it from the closes garbage cans. Now the shoes on my feet might be too big because I am such a small man but understand unlike you I was taken from my home land and brought to this land. See I have picked cotton and I have stood face to face with the white man. I've have had my own business which was taken from under my hands.

And I have shared a tear or two. Cursed God just like any other man; had my family taken away to never see them again but I can't expect you to understand because in your eyes I am a nobody just another Black man standing here on this corner with a bible in my hand.

A. L. WATKINES

MAMA'S LOVE
FOR ME

For nine hold months within her womb she carried me, feed and nurtured me. From the seed my father planted within her to create me. Not a drop of liquor or drugs touched her body.

For it was her wish to be the best mother she could be unlike some of her girlfriends she wanted everyone to know she loved me and that she was proud to have me. When I was born she breastfeed, washed and took care of me.

Then one day in her church she took me before her pastor and God to have him baptized me at that time I was of the age of three. Each night before I would go to sleep she read the bible and said my prayers with me then wrapped her arms around me as if she was protecting me from the ghost to be and not letting any harm come to me.

Each morning as I went off to school from her bedroom window I could she her watching me as this big yellow bus pulled to pick up me. Some days she would come up to the school and pick up me just to walk with me home she called it her quiet time with me. Along the way we would stop in the park and I would sit upon a swing and she would push me and then she would lay upon the grass with me. Then we would go home and she would cook dinner and help me with my homework.

Now I am grown and just like me, mother she is still wiping my tears from my face and looking out her bedroom window as I leave for work each day. Sometimes she might even come on my job to have lunch with me then her and my son and I will sit by the water for a while. Then she will push him upon a swing as she used to do me we will lay in the grass talk about our dreams.

THE BEST OF BOTH WORLDS

MAMA'S LOVE
FOR ME

See my mother is now at the beautiful age of eighty-three
and for nine whole months within her womb she carried me.

A. L. WATKINES

MR. APPLESAUCES' LOUNGE

Now the word was all over town for tonight was the opening of Mr. Applesauce lounge. For weeks, poster and signs had been placed all up and down Watermelon Street. Early today outside the lounge you could hear the disc jockey, Ms Peaches preparing her music with its own beat.

Early today the janitor had came in and sat up the table and chairs and at that very moment the stage was being prepared for tonight two new singing groups were going to have their day big show Mr. Chicken Tenders and Buffalo Wings and Ms. Hamburger Pizza with her band Mac & Cheese. Now the owner Mr. Steak and his friends Mr. Pork Chop and Mrs. Sweet Green Peas had invested all their money to fulfill their one and only dream - tonight's grand opening. Now the bartenders Mr. Ham Hock and Ms. Collard Green had came in the night before to make sure their bar was sit up and completed. The waiters Mr. Corn and Mr. Red Beans was coming in around noon to pick up their suits for the evening; the waitresses Ms. Eggs and Ms. Meat Loaf with Ms. Bacon - these sisters was fine as could be and they had came in earlier this morning to pick up their blouses and dresses to fit over those bodies for any man could see then took them to Mr. Ham's cleaner to be pressed and cleaned.

Now Mr. TV Dinner and Mr. Oatmeal were to greet and meet people at the door. And although they might not be needed, the bouncers were the Catfish brothers, would be there and ready. And if by chance one of the groups was unable to make it, there was Mr. Baby Back Ribs and his band.

THE BEST OF BOTH WORLDS

MR. APPLESAUCES' LOUNGE

Well the time had come and Mr. & Mrs. Shrimp was the first to enter the door, then came Mr. Turkey with Ms Mashed Potatoes, and they went right to the dance floor. After them was the Chocolate Chip brother and sister - they had made reservations the night before and outside still waiting was Mr. Taco, with Mr. Beef Stew and Mr. Green String Beans at the front door. Now behind them you could see the Baked Ham family alone with Mr. Mustard and Mr. Turnip Greens. The news was there to cover the opening with one of its reporter Mr. Black Eye Peas. It was told that later that night radio disc jockey, Mr. Grit, was going to broadcast from there. Now over in a far away corner of the lounge you could see Mr. Chicken Soup and Ms. Kellogg Froot Loops and they were having some fun. Someone said they saw the Peanut Butter twins there along with Ms. Wheat and White Bread they were sisters.

Well all night long the music was banging and the place was filled; the camera man Mr. Jell-O and his girlfriend Ms. Jelly were taking some very beautiful picture shots. The place was sold out but outside the door there was another sign that said "We will blow your mind tomorrow night, see performing tomorrow night will be Ms. Strawberry Shortcake and the Butter Pecan Band and Also Mr. Blackberry Band".

Now Mr. Chittling and Mr. Pig Feet will be meeting and greeting people at the door and Mrs. Whiting Fish and Ms. Beef Rib, Mr. Okra and Mr. Neck bone waiting the floors. Now Mr. Black Coffee will be the first disc jockey and then

later Mrs. Sweet Potato Pie will take the floor, and on the dance floor you will find Mr. Liver and Mrs. Sweet Tea and you can see Mr. Thanksgiving Dressing. And Ms., Banana Pudding doing their favorite dances, all at Mr. Applesauce's Lounge.

A. L. WATKINES

WHAT HAS COME OVER ME

At this very time and very moment I can't seem to understand what has come over me. See I have always been a strong man, but when I get around you I find myself becoming very weak and yet there is something about you, in more ways than one, that seem to bring out the best within me. It seems as if when I am with you, I see a part of me that I have never seen before. Yet never has a woman done these kinds of things to me. You're unlike any other woman before you. Could it be that God has chosen you for me in a world where the love of a good woman is like finding money growing from a tree. Could it be the delicate way you carry yourself? The delicate woman that excited the inner man within me, or could it be the voluptuous way your body, hips and thighs move in those tight fitting jeans, or maybe those sun dresses that you wear that make your body look all so complete, could it be the peach colored complexion of your skin.

That always seem to tempt me, I know maybe it's the wisdom and knowledge you have that tickles the thought of you being my woman inside of me, or could it be the smell of your perfume that projects itself from your body into the air about me, or is it the strong black richness of your hair. Could it be that I see within all the women that I need and yet it could be gentle sound that seems to command the attention of a man, or could it be the look of love that is within your eyes that I see, or just maybe it's the intelligent strong ambitious and dynamic woman I see who is, at times weak, now could it be that to look upon your beauty causes men to fall at your feet or maybe it is your motherly instinct or the need for a love that will make you complete. But my beloved, however, whatever it is about you that has taken a bite out of me, I find myself giving it a standing ovation. Always my beautiful black queen.

THE BEST OF BOTH WORLDS

LAST NIGHT

Last night I had a dream unlike any other dream and in that dream I felt the spirit of someone watching over me. Now in that dream I had my life laid out for me like footsteps in the sand. I could see the road that was meant for me laid out before me. But as I ran to place my feet in the footsteps before me something kept holding and pulling back on me to the point I could not break free.

And yet, I could hear a voice calling out to me so I cried out with a loud voice "Let go of me" but no answer did I receive and whatever it was it was still holding me for it was like glue stuck to my rear.

Yes, last night I had a dream unlike any other dream and in that dream I felt the spirit of someone walking along side me. When I would take one step they would take two steps in front of me. So I ran to see their face but their back was all that I could see. Again I cried out "Stop" but no reply did I receive.

Last night I had a dream unlike any other dream. In that dream I felt the spirit of someone praying for me unlike any other prayer I had ever received. In that dream I witnessed tears running down their cheeks and I could see them fighting with the Devil to save my soul and set me free. So I cried out, "Satan get thee behind me!"

So I jumped up out of my bed and in the shadows a small face appeared. Before I had clearly opened my eyes the face disappeared right before me. So, I quickly closed my eyes again hoping that I might regain that dream, but I found myself falling into a deep sleep.

Yes last night I had a dream unlike any other dream. In that dream I felt a spirit calling out to me. So I replied "Yes Lord what you will have of me". Again no answer did I receive. I tried to make out the voice as it again spoke unto me.

A. L. WATKINES

LAST NIGHT

It was so far from me that I could not hear it clearly but within my mind I will never forget the words that were spoken to me. For it said, "Trust in God and believe that He will supply all your needs".

So tonight when I close my eyes I hope to again have a few more dreams. But there is no question in my mind that it is my Mother, Brother and Grandmother watching over me. It could also just be God wrapping His arms lovingly around me.

THE BEST OF BOTH WORLDS

MY STRONG
BLACK SISTERS

Stand up my strong black sisters in Christ
For God has removed the splendor from within your eyes
He has given you the power to no longer cry over the pains of human life

So won't you open your eyes and see now is your time to live
A life as He would have you to be

Don't let the Devil steal your joy with lies or your thought of living a Christian life

Stand up my strong black sisters in Christ
Tell me have you said your prayers tonight
Why do you keep questioning God as to why?
When He's asking you to let Him be the head of your life
For He said judge no man with the human eye but look into his heart for the heart doesn't lie

Stand up my strong black sisters in Christ
learn to hold your Godly head up high
know that you have favor within Gods' eyes

Speak those things that you're holding back inside because those same words might give someone else a peace of mine or even save their life stand up and know that God is by your side when man turns his back on you and fill your heart and mine with lies

Understand when I tell you to stand up my strong black sisters in Christ. For God says it's your time to reap the fruit of the vine

Don't let the Devil deny you your right to the tree of life
Won't you read your Bible tonight?

A. L. WATKINES

MY STRONG BLACK SISTERS

For it says forgive those whom has hurt you
and those with whom you have hurt them within their eyes
As well as those whom have cause you pain and strife
For if you can not forgive them how can you ask God to
forgive you tonight

Remember that I told you today
That the splendor has been removed from your eyes
Ask God to help you put away your worldly pride

For now that you have wisdom and knowledge
Or are you just wasting yours and Gods' time
If so why don't just ask him to let you die
For how can you have wisdom and not let it lead your life
my strong black sisters in Christ

Remember the fight is not ours to fight
For nothing comes free in life and that two wrongs don't
make a right Confess your sins to Him and ask Him to look
within your heart tonight and let Him be your light

For the heart is a home for love
Remember that worry and anger is a sin in Gods' eyes
Won't you let His joy and peace come into your life?
Tonight my sisters baptize your body, soul and mind in Christ

THE BEST OF BOTH WORLDS

NEVER LIKED THICK WOMEN

Never been one who liked a thick woman always felt they were too much for me to hold. Too much loving for me to give or receive. See I am a slim kind of fellow.

Don't feel I needed that much loving to make me feel whole and yet to make love with a thick woman would be hard to roll around with my the living room or bedroom floor.

But today I saw a thick woman who could bring any man to his knees with his face on the floor whether she was slim, middle built or thick as can be now her hair was curly and down to her shoulders in the right side of her nose she wore a nose ring.

Her body shape was unearthly good from the crown of her head to her toes. The way her hips moved had every man on the bus face in the window watching her walk down the street.

Now I must admit I have seen many women but this one had beauty untold it was not hard to see, with just one look she had the power to stop traffic but that day just like with so many other men words to her was hard for me to speak.

Never been one who liked thick women always felt they were too much for me see I am a slim kind of fellow and only petite women will understand a man like me.

But today I saw this woman and a new spirit was born within me I would have loved the chance to meet her one on one for just one chance to see if she was what God had for me.

A. L. WATKINES

PEOPLE ALWAYS ASK ME!

For some reason I had you on my mind today so I took the timeout to write this for you see.......

People always ask me what I want in a woman. I want a woman in which we both will never grow old. A woman who will intoxicate me like my favorite glass of white wine to drink not with her body but with her mind. A woman who will intoxicate me with the warmth of her heart and the goodness within her.

I want a woman with whom her words will have the power to bring me to my knees. When she expresses her love for me and yet she will remain to be the woman God made her to be. I want a woman who knows how to love a man as she loves God and herself that unseen kind of love. Yet her beauty is not only just on the outside but the inside too.

I want a woman who is an idol in the eyes of those she meet and not a holier then thou kind of woman using the verses of the Bible every time she speaks. See I have not got there yet and is still working on me. I want a woman who knows what love is and not just the meaning of the words. A woman who is giving of herself as Jesus gave Himself and not seeking only material things. A woman who knows that God will not give her any 'junk'.

I want a woman who is silly and will laugh at my jokes even when they might not be funny. A woman whose lips are made in Heaven with the taste of honey. I want a woman who can be freaky in the bedroom and a woman in the streets.

A woman who has a body that would make a blind man begs God for eyes to see along with a voice that would sound like an Angel when she speaks.

PEOPLE ALWAYS ASK ME!

A woman who will bring joy to my heart just by her saying hello. Tell me am I asking too much or am I am dreaming. I want a woman who has let go of her past or the mistakes other men has made towards her. A woman who will walk besides me, not in front of me or in back of me. Most of all a woman who can talk to me about anything freely. I want a woman who will besides me when the ways of the world become too much for me. She will remind me that she is there as my armor to help me.

..........Understand this is what I am looking for; now after reading this you might think I am dreaming maybe even crazy but all that I am asking for I can bring the same to the table. So I need you to know that my mind was filled with the thoughts of talking with you this evening and hoping to get to know the woman within you.

A. L. WATKINES

SOMETIMES

Sometimes I wondered if there is something wrong with me. I look for love and yet love seems to over look me.

I know I have done wrong and I was not the man God may have wanted me to be but what does that have to do with someone loving me.

I find myself asking Lord why me then I look for an answer, but I just remain on my knees.

I know they say you reap what you sow and this I do believe but I don't know if I can do this lonely thing .

I tried to do it my way to find the woman of my dreams and yet I have only found those who want to use me.

So now I will try to do it God's way, for there is no other way left for me to see I used to think I had it all and the best of everything.

But like so many times before I was only fooling me, so my question today is why life has played this trick on me.
How I find myself stealing from Paul to pay Peter every other week?

How sometimes I come close to love and other times love comes close to me but we never seem to met in the middle that's the way it seems to always.

So sometimes I wonder is there something wrong with me for I have a heart and blood does run through me and yet love seems to over look me.

Seems like the Devil always plays with me and yet I know the words to sweep a woman off her feet and turn her head to the point she will take a second look at me.

Sometimes I wonder is there something wrong within me…

THE BEST OF BOTH WORLDS

THE COLOR OF CHOCOLATE MILK

She was the color of sweet chocolate milk. Rich, sweet and in her voice I could hear the sound of her African accent speaking so beautifully. Now her body was slim and some would say she was petite but I must admit she was built right for me.

The smile upon her face was that of the sun rising up over old oak trees. Her eyes were hazel brown with the power to weaken a man from his head down to his feet. Her lips seem to move as gently as she chews on some gum sitting in her seat with her legs crossed showing their full beauty.

Now her hair was black to her shoulders, mixed with gold highlights and in one of her ear lobes she wore a gold earring. The movement of her body was like watching a race car win its race. Just looking at her brought a joyful smile to my face sometimes I wondered how God could make someone in such a special way and keep her hidden away.

The perfume smell of her body was that of a rose opening its leaves on the first day. How I wish that I could tell you more but she pulled the bus line cord and begin to walk away. But there in the windows of the bus you could see every man on the bus face even the bus driver had to stop to take another look before he drove away. I must admit, I was thirty and would have loved to partake of a drink of that chocolate milk that got away from me that day. For she was the color of chocolate milk - rich and sweet!

A. L. WATKINES

WENT TO THE RIVER

Went to the river this morning like I always do because I wanted to have a drink because the weather was hot more than usual. As I bent over to get a drink of water, my face in the water I did not see. For it was not myself that I saw and there was something different about me.

I saw the man that I used to be - selfish, jealous, and angry. All this was in my face right before me. Back in the past, I believed the world owed something to me after all the pain and hut it had caused me, but I was only fooling myself.

Went to the river this morning like I always do because I wanted to have a drink because the weather was hot more than usual. As I bent over to get a drink of water, my face in the water I did not see. There stood a face of a sinful man looking up at me. See I used to let women, cars and money have full control over me and I forgot God's word that states you shall have no other God before Him.

Now in that same water, again my face I showed a liar, thief and the man who robbed God right in front of me. I felt tears run down my checks and something inside of me moved unlike I had never seen.

Went to the river this morning like I always do because I wanted to have a drink because the weather was hot more than usual. As I bent over to get a drink of water, my face in the water I did not see. What I saw inside of me was hurt and pain so I looked a little deeper then I saw the Devil within me.

Now it was right there and then that I felled on bended knees. At that very moment I asked God what He wanted of me and what it is that He saw within me. Then I asked Him if He would save me and what must I do to be set free from all these people I see within me. It was there at the water that day He baptized me.

So this morning, when I went to the river to get a drink of water God gave me a drink.

THE BEST OF BOTH WORLDS

TODAY I FELT A TEAR

Today I felt a tear run down my face. I wondered to myself what caused it. For it felt so good upon my face. For I had just read my bible and it spoke of God's mercy and grace. Right after reading that I begin to pray.

Now I asked Him for forgiveness and to remove my bitterness and hate. Then I asked Him for more understanding and to teach me to love my enemies anyway. See I asked Him to touch my heart in His own special way and it was then that I felt that tear come running down my face.

And it was then that I begin to thank Him for letting me witness another day. Because all my family and loved ones have all passed away and I had no one to encourage me along my way.

Today I felt a tear run down my face. I wondered to myself what caused it for it felt so good upon my face. Yet there was no sadness on my mind, any anger or hate but there was this tear that I felt running down my face.

It was nothing that I was laughing about and there was nothing silly that someone said. There were no special memories that ran across my mind to cause me to feel this way. For there was nothing about today that was special or for that matter yesterday that what can I say.

It was then that I remembered how He seemed to always make a way out of no way. Even when I refused to believe in Him, He still held open Heaven Gates.

Sometimes I wondered how He still has favor in me when there's doubt in my mind day after day.

TODAY I FELT
A TEAR

I remembered why I felt that tear running down my face. For I never had anyone to love me this way; I believed until that day and if I did I would have not known it anyway.

See I never knew how to love myself so I asked Him to teach me the right way. It was right then that He told me to look inside myself and begin to have faith. And it was right then that I begin to give Him praise.

Now I remembered why I felt that tear run down my face. For I now know what caused it. It was God washing my sadness away.

THE BEST OF BOTH WORLDS

PRIME BEEF

Look at me I am a strong black man
From my head to my feet
Pure prime beef

The finest of clothes
And the best of shoes on my feet,
Every man wishes he could be me

Look at me, a strong black man
A cup of coffee mixed with a touch of cream
Rich in wisdom, knowledge
And full of hopes and dreams

Hair cut short and eyes as brown
As the sun rising over the moonlit sea

Full of love and yet
Not too tall to be short
But built with a body that's willing to please

Now I am no player no gigolo
Those kind of men are not in me
But understand my sister
I only want to be the man my mother raised me to be
And the man God wants me to be

Yes, look at me
I am a strong black man
From my head down to my feet

And yet at times, I am as lonely as can be
Like I said before, I look for love
And yet love walks right past me

Maybe I am asking for too much
When I say I want someone to love me for me

A. L. WATKINES

PRIME BEEF

Just like so many others
I have done some things
That I might not be able to hold my head up
But God has forgiven me

There were times
When I did not know love
And yes it was right in front of me

And there were times
Just like so many others
I look out just for me

But look at me today
You would not see those things in me
As the old saying goes
I'm not the same man I used to be

So look at me I am a strong black man
And yes, I might be missing a few teeth
And the gray that was once my hair
You can no longer see

My lips might be small
And my feet a size twelve
But again, my shoes look good on me
And it's true, I might be very quiet
The first time we meet

Yet I am a strong black man
From my head down to my feet
Made from my mothers' love
Created by my fathers' sperm seed.

THE BEST OF BOTH WORLDS

THAT NIGHT

I got in my car stuck in the keys and turned it to the right. When before my eyes I saw the check engine light. So I rushed it to the dealer and he kept it over night. When I went to get the car and again stuck in the key this time I witnessed the gas light came on.

I drove slowly to the nearest gas station to fill it up with unleaded gas that night. Before I could drive away I got a flat tire on the right side. Now I didn't want to leave it so I get on bended knees hoping to do the job right. I changed that old flat tire.

I got back into my car, turned on the engine and to my delight it started right up but there was a bang-bang on the left side. I went to drive away there was anger within my eyes. See I had made a special date with my woman who was the love of my life.

She had brought a new dress, got her nails and hair done just right. She had even sprayed on some of her perfume earlier that day so I knew she would smell out of sight.

As I begin to drive off I saw smoke coming from the muffler and I must admit it was so thick I had to pull over to the side.

Now I sit there wondering why things had to happen on special this night and it was then that I remembered God does things in his own time.

See a bad accident happened on the road that I was on that night which killed six people. If I would have kept our date we might not have lived to see the next night.

A. L. WATKINES

SISTER I PROMISE

The Lord is my Shepherd and I shall not want, but my sister, I promise I would like to get to know you. Maybe take you out to dinner and show you off for the world to see the gift that God has given me.

Let me show you the man God made this brother to be. Massage your mind with the wisdom God has put inside of me.

Let me share with you my knowledge of what I believe a woman should be. Then dance with you over the joy that He has given me.

Let me teach you that God says He will supply all our needs. Even get down on my knees and pray with you that in each other arms we will always be.

Let me help you understand that my charms are not a line to you, but are what I feel inside when I think of us, for my sister you look so good to me.

Understand I would like to taste your lips in hopes that they would remind me of when my mother first gave me sweets.

See I promise never to deceive you I will always be a gentleman if you let me. I'll show you how Adam felt when he first woke and saw Eve. For my sister, your beauty is so complete. I'll place you in a garden were the world will always be surrounded by you, God and me; I'll show you a love that has never before been seen.

I'll take you and sit you on a throne that will read "God's Gift to Me" and other women shall be envious and other brothers shall desire to be blessed like me.

Sister, I promise for the Lord is my Shepherd and I shall not want for within you He has fulfilled all my needs.

THE BEST OF BOTH WORLDS
MY SPECIAL NUBIAN QUEEN

My Special Nubian Queen:

In this letter to you, I need you to understand that I once was young and foolish when it came to the needs and wants of a woman. Now I am older and am learning to appreciate all that I see within a woman like you.

It is written that the steps of a good man are ordered by God. He is delighted to see a good man that will love you as he love's God. Even though he shall fall like all men do he shall not be cast down for God will up hold him.

See, a good lover is a man, not a boy in the body of a man. A good lover and good loving is more than having the ability to hold your hips and waist within my hands – morning, noon or night - making over powering love to you. It is seeking to know what is within your mind; seeking to understand your feelings and your needs as a woman. It is the ability to see you in the eyes of God and not in the eyes of a worldly man.

For the word of God says that I should love you as Christ loves the church; good loving is the ability to enjoy your entire companion in your past and present life from the crown of their head to their feet and cry no more.

It is not letting them be a God over you and keep you from loving another with all your heart and soul because this one did you wrong. It is that step of faith that the bible speaks of because you are willing to step out on faith. When it comes to God then you must be willing to step out on faith because he knows what best for you when it comes to a love one.

Good loving is the ability to be a lover during the day as well as the night. A good lover is someone who knows your feelings without you having to tell them or share with them. It is the ability to join together as one accord but good loving is also the ability to get over our past mistakes by seeking a new start within yourself - setting yourself free from you.

A. L. WATKINES

MY SPECIAL NUBIAN QUEEN

It's wanting to be a part of the other persons' healing, it's rebuilding their and yourself and it is not trying to do it on your own but together.

As I sit here writing this who would have ever thought I would have survived my past and find you. So many times when the thought of a relationship or a female friendship would come my way, I was the first to run. Although within my mind I was telling myself I want these things.

As you read this within your mind you might be saying I don't even know you as the world should. See today we live more for the world and less for ourselves; to say these things but understand I don't live my life for the world.

You as a woman have pulled life back into me simply by making me laugh. I enjoy the times we talk but most of all I enjoy the woman I see within you. As a woman you have opened my blind eyes so once again I can see the one thing that I once refused the most and my heart is overwhelmed.

I have found myself now when I think about loving myself; I find myself thinking about how to enjoy you for you have become my minister. My desire is to be there for you as a friend and to heat your soul when things seem cold.

You are the spiritual song I sing in the early part of the morning and the closing at night. See I want to be your instrument of peace that is a special part of you, believe it or not you are the reason that I am here. God brings people into our lives for a reason and it more about you then me.

Now if you need me I will be whatever you need me to be. For you are that light in the darkness of the night that the world now seeks so freely and openly and with that feeling I feel I can count on you.

MY SPECIAL NUBIAN QUEEN

No matter what anyone says you're God gift to me - at the right time for me. Forgive me because my desire is to someday live the remaining of my life with the love of my life and these kinds of feeling are new to me. Truthfully they have really knocked me off my feet, catching me off guard, blindsiding me and it has gotten to the point that I just got to tell somebody. I am like the blind man at the temple when Jesus opened his eyes.

I just have to share what you have done in my life with others and not care what they might think because we fit together like a hand to a glove. In so many ways you understand me when I say that I would have never thought that I would have found Heaven here on Earth. And yet there were times when I thought that God would not forgive me for my wrongs yet in this short time you have given me what I needed the most by showing me Gods' favor on me by entrusting me with not only your friendship but your willingness to share with me your wisdom.

Things that no other woman ever offered me before; maybe it was that I would not let it come into my life, but in my mind you are worth going to the alter for in prayer. My special Nubian Queen we seem to communicate so will and I want to learn to love you from my side of life and how to light the fire and wisdom inside of you. Understand this is not a game, please; take this down within your soul.

A. L. WATKINES

COURT OF
THE MOST HIGH

You my brother and sister have been accused of bombarding God with your prayers while forgetting others you might know who are in need of prayers.

Therefore you are hear by ordered by this Court to be sentenced to a long Life and Prosperity with no Bail or an Appeal. For today, you have been labeled Blessed and Highly Favored and hear by detained in God's custody Forever...Amen

For today you have been detained by this court to make it and you shall surely achieve all your goals and all that God has for you. He will supply all that you need if you are willing to step back and just believe. There is nothing too hard for God. For you must remember that God can open doors that man has closed and He can close doors that man has opened.

If you believe in sorrow, look back to where He has brought you from. If you believe in worry, look around you and see what this world has become. But if you believe in faith, keep looking up for we know not the day or the hour that He will return. Yet we must learn to ask God to grant us patience to endure our blessing no matter when the blessings might come. For God's time is not always our time.

Therefore you have been sentenced to be faithful as a child of the most high. Remember that He gave His only Son so that you might have life.

THE BEST OF BOTH WORLDS

ARE YOU HUNGRY?

Understand me when I say that I like it when life is like a buffet and you can eat upon your own experiences, and with every passing day of life, the menu seem to change to something different every day and no matter how you try, it never seems to be the same.

Now we know with life we might sometimes enjoy what is on the menu for that day. We have good and bad days and then there are the times in which you may not enjoy the menu of that day. Because on that day you are faced with challenges that make you feel that you are at a crossroads. These feelings may cause you to make decisions in which you find yourself just needing some encouragement or some advice.

It could be that sometimes it's good to have a different focus, a different outlook, because sometime people can see things within us that we can not see within ourselves. Sometime we just need a reminder of where we have been in life and where we have come from. As well as what we have gone through to get where we are.

Now, I have always been told that God knows our needs before we speak them to Him and that He knows our heart. So, during my moment of need and direction I reflect back to "where I started from".

Just thinking with some of the wisdom and introspection that has given me a different perspective, enlightenment and inspiration. Most of all, He's given me time to think back on the quotes that were passed down to me by my grandmother and grandfather. Even those moments of quotes from my mother and father.

Let me not forget the people across the street that caused me to hold my head up high. They helped me back then, to see where I was going with my life, with quotes like "a great mind discuss ideas and an average mind discuss events" or "most small minds discuss people", "don't be afraid of greatness because some people are born to be great and some people achieve greatness and than there are those who have greatness thrust upon them'.

Therefore even if you're on the right track in life you will get run over if you just sit back and wait for things to come to you. Understand great spirits had always encountered violent opposition from mediocre minds.

THE BEST OF BOTH WORLDS

BLINDED BY DARKNESS

A THIEF IN THE NIGHT

Somebody stop her I've been robbed by a thief in the night. See in my mind I've held her over a hundred times and in my mind I have tasted her lips upon mines. My eyes have looked into hers and her world has over taken me like a bottle of sweet white wine.

For in my mind her beauty has over powered me unlike the beauty of any other woman that has been placed before me. To me she is a gift for the world to see. Within my mind she is everything that any real man would want his woman to be but remember this is all within my mind.

For in my mind her hair reminds me of black silk sheets. Yet in my mind being loved by her can be the best thing next to God moving within me. For sometimes in my mind I have made love to her a thousand times. As I've tossed and turned within my sheets only to wake up and find it was only a dream. In my mind the smell of her perfume has comforted me even when it was only my cologne that I smelled around me.

For in my mind she is an Angel sent to share the rest of my life with me. She is a welcome change from all of the other women I have had the honor of meeting. Who only wanted marital things, and yet in my mind I see with in her the sun rising over a clear ocean sea and a star sent to watch over me. She is the new song that I sing.

For in my mind I find myself asking God to let her be all the woman that I need. In my mind I have touched her, walked with her, cried with her and shared laughs with her. I have also given my heart to her - all these things are within my mind as she has become a thief in the night.

THE BEST OF BOTH WORLDS

HOLE IN THE WALL

Walked into this hole in the wall the other night yet something in the atmosphere felt not right. Now the DJ was playing the blues as I looked around no seat could be found. As this big large bouncer took my money and asked me to please move forward.

So I walked to the bar to get a better look at the women sitting around the dance floor. I ordered a drink - see I was just going to have one and go.

But then my stomach started crying out from the smell of that chicken coming from the kitchen door. I sat down to have a bit and then in my mind I was ready to go when this fine sexy sister asked me to come with her to the dance floor. As all the other men within the place eyes felled to the floor.

This time the DJ was playing an old favorite love song and everyone was moving slow. See this woman took me in her arms and held me as if I was someone she already known and no man could ask for more.

Now her body felt so good next to mine. That I wanted to just escort her right out the door. But before I knew it there was no more room on the dance floor and I must admit the movement of her body next to mine made me cry out with joy. I wanted to slip the DJ ten dollars to play just one more song, see I no longer wanted to go home.

Soon I found myself looking into her eyes - I tell you nothing could have dragged me off the floor then I found myself kissing her lips. A burning desire came over my soul for I was kissing on a woman that I didn't even know yet her lips reminded me of sex. So within my mind I was seeking and asking for more but just as I was about to get closer to her I heard someone whisper to her your man has just walked through the door.

A. L. WATKINES

HOLE IN
THE WALL

Now I thought it was only right to end our dancing on the floor but as I tried to break it off, but she held me even closer. Now it was not long after I felt a tap on my shoulder and the next time I looked up I was getting up off the floor.

See I told myself I went into this place because my friends called it a disco. But to me my fondest memories of this place were that I was able to get off the dance floor in this hole in the wall night club.

THE BEST OF BOTH WORLDS

I HEARD THEM MAKING LOVE

I heard them making love the other night in the room next door to me. The sound that came from that woman voice put chills all over me.

For he seemed to be loving her somewhat tenderly and with each stroke he seemed never to miss a beat. Now the sound of their two lips kissing seemed to bring back memories.

There was even a time when I heard her groan and other times she let out a scream. Now it sounded so good it was to the point at times I cried out with her.

Then it soon got quiet and I told myself they had fallen asleep. But before I could close my eyes real good I heard him cry out "Baby girl give it to me" and that old brass bed begin to once again shake.

Now I want to hit on the wall just to let them know it was getting to me. But deep within my mind I was jealous because it was not me.

So I turned on the television hoping that the sound of her joy would not awake those special feeling inside of me. See last night my woman and I had a fight; so I jumped into my car and came to the hotel to get some sleep.

Now how was I to know that they would be getting it on all night next door to me? Then after a while I heard the shower come on and my heart felt at ease. I knew that their entire love making had come to an end and in my mind I wanted some sleep.

Soon after that I heard them laughing as the door to their room opened gently so they could leave.

A. L. WATKINES

I HEARD THEM MAKING LOVE

And because she had sounded so good I rushed to the window just to get a peek. Now baby girls' body was banging - well put together and complete.

 As I laid my head upon my pillow my mind begun to dream for I will always remember that I heard them making love the other night in the room next door to me.

THE BEST OF BOTH WORLDS

MEN OF COLOR

Men of color never fear the beauty of a woman nor her status, her thoughts or her belief. Because perhaps she's been hurt by some other man of color when it was love that she was seeking.

Now the soft words that you may say at this time might bring comfort to her ears. Although she may turn away right now those same words someday she may long to hear.

Understand, my man of color as long as God is by your side and is your guide. Know that the beauty of a woman doesn't lie within her skin, her body but within her mind. For it has been said that the price of a true woman had far more value of rubies just because she is virtuous.

Men of color look and see that a woman's heart should be so hidden in Christ that a man should seek Christ first in order to find her.

Men of color never fear the mate that God has in store for you is just a breath away - for you will be her Adam and she your Eve.

Men of color listen to God and not your heart. Hear the words that He speaks for He knows your heart and your every need better than you.

Men of color look into your heart then look into your soul and mirror. Then tell me what you see. Is the love of God within your heart? Or is it the lust that's in a woman of color your seeking.

A. L. WATKINES

SHE WAS GHETTO

They said she was ghetto and a ghetto woman is all she will ever be. See the woman was from the hood part of the city street. No matter where she would go people know it because of the way she would speak - for her voice was loud and she always had to be heard or seen.

Now they say the woman could fight; she should have been a boxer fighting in a ring for she could just about beat any brother down that she might meet. It was said she was a mother with two children or maybe it was three. They say she used all kind of drugs even sold her body to supply all her needs. And yet she never completed school she was one year from getting her high school degree.

Now she got knock up by some young man and he made her a woman of the street. He would beat her as if she was nothing. Because of that she disrespected her mother, took her children's shoes off their feet, and left them in her apartment naked and with nothing there to eat.

Some say she could have been somebody special but all she knew was the ways of the streets. Stealing and lying to her family while wanting to be somebody she could never be with. Loud music playing there she was standing high on the corner street even the police felt sorry for her so they would just let her be.

With holes in her blue jeans nothing but skin and bones was all that you could see. With sandals on her feet for shoes she wore winter, summer and spring. Her hair was nappy like a bird nest reaching it peak.

The smell from her body would make you lose your thoughts for something to eat. Some said that she had gone crazy but she was just as smart as can be she had a business mind but she was ghetto from the street.

THE BEST OF BOTH WORLDS

HAVE YOU EVER WITNESSED?

Have you ever witnessed a man being hung on a tree his only crime was to want to know how to read and write? And yet there was some who died because of their belief.

Have you ever witnessed a man being hung on a tree because of his religion and the God in which he believed? Tell me have you every witnessed a man being hung on a tree because he refuse to work a job for his master seven days out of the week then whipped and chained then feed nothing to eat because he refused to work.

Please tell me have you ever witnessed a man being hung on a tree because of the land he brought or was given once he was what this world called free.

Have you ever witnessed a man being hung from a tree because his greatest desire was to someday be called or have someone say he was free in a world where he was looked upon as less than a human?

Tell me have you ever witnessed a man being hung just because of the color of his skin is it a curse from God that we can't all be the same are we descended of Able or is it Cain.

Have you ever witness a man being hung on a tree because of his ability to speak and bring together nations seeking peace. That not only one race but every race of man, woman and children could reach their dreams.

See I have witness all these things seven days a week for it's in the newspapers, on the radio and even in the books I read. It's even in the jobs as a race of people looked around it's even on my neighborhood streets.

It's in the school, the jail, prisons; even with the police see we are surrounded by prejudice only now they have put on suits and dresses to replace their white sheets.

SLIM AND PETITE

She was a slim and petite little thing of a woman. I must tell you that this Black woman was mean. Now in her younger days, I do believe she was looked upon as a Queen. Understand me, when I say that just to look upon her and to look at her body form – you can tell she was every man's dream of how he wanted his woman to be.

Now her eyes seemed to speak the word of sex if you know what I mean. The sound of her voice was like that of an Angel singing with the choir before God on bended knees. Her long black hair, although, I must admit some of it was weave stood out like black pearls found in the deep ocean sea.

Yet her well but slender shaped hips made her desirable in those tight blue jeans. There in her sweater two hill tops could be seen upon her chest unlike anything a man could ever dream.

Now upon her right hand she wore this overwhelming diamond ring and when she was asked about it her words were always this "old thing". Now the color of her skin was that of a hot cup of tea with just a touch of lemon and drop of cream. If given the chance with the right man she would be willing to slip into his dreams.

THE BEST OF BOTH WORLDS

TURNED ON THE
RADIO THIS MORNING

I was driving in my car had my feelings on my mind
Thought I had it all together, thought my life was going just fine.

Then this song came on the radio
That one song that always bring tears to my eyes
for the singer of the song was an old friend of mines.

He said, "If you think your lonely now wait until tonight."
It was then and there that I felt the need to asked God why?
for I knew I had done some wrong and I had broken some hearts in my time but that was all in my past and that was all in my younger life. Never though I would reap what I had put out in the past.

See I turned on the radio this morning had my feelings on my mind something last night just was not right there was a storm brewing in my mind. I thought I had it all together thought my life was going just fine.

But this song on the radio just seemed to blow my mind to the point I rushed to change the station but the words of the song some how seemed to stay on my mind telling my heart to keep my faith alive.

Now I wondered if god was punishing me or if this was all in my mind. I wondered why I have been alone for what seemed like two lifetimes. I never knew this was God's and my time.

I wondered if I would ever be happy or just grow old alone
I wondered what I could do to change things see I've prayed a hundred times as to why life be so unkind.

Yes I turned on the radio this morning had my feelings on my mind something last night just was not right there was a storm brewing in my mind. When the song on the radio made me question God as to whether He had turned His back on me at this time in my life.

A. L. WATKINES

THEY CALLED HIM VIPER

They called him a viper. A man more deceiving than any creature or beast.

God placed him upon this Earth as a human being. Now he is able to manipulate both men and women with the greatest of ease. Understand this man doesn't only do his deceiving from within a tree; he can stand right before you and not blink an eye as he did his thing.

Some people question God as to how a man's heart could be so mean. Was he born that way or was he raised that way? He was charming and loving and some might say he was gentle when he needed to be. But if you took a good look within his eyes, you could see he would take you for everything.

His voice was like a preacher, I tell you the man could speak and he was dynamic in the way that he would speak. But when he was finished you would believe he had the power to part an ocean or a sea.

He was a well dressed man and the smell of his body was like that of a dew drop falling from a tree leaf. The way this man carried himself you would believe that he had the highest college degree but the sixth grade was the highest education he completed.

He never learned to write or read and all his teachings came from remembering things. He drove an old broken down car that he kept washed and cleaned and he lived in an old wooden shack in the dangerous part of the city to the point he kept a loaded gun in his house under his mattress.

Understand he had no job, social security income was all that he received. He had no wife and children. They say this man was too mean and if Satan had a son this man would fit the tee.

THE BEST OF BOTH WORLDS

THEY CALLED
HIM VIPER

For they called him a viper. A man more deceiving than any creature or beast. The story goes on but we will pick it up next week.

A. L. WATKINES

SOMEBODY HIT ME

I was walking home today when somebody hit me but when I turned around I saw only my shadow behind me. I walked a little more and I tell you the truth I felt somebody hit me again. See this time it was so hard that I almost felt off my feet. All last night I fought with the Devil and this morning his thoughts had over powered me.

See I was about to do something silly because my mind was confused and depression was getting the best of me. So I pulled myself together, turned around and made sure there was no body walking behind me. See it was right then when I made one more step again somebody hit me.

So I tried to walk backwards I don't know what was going on in my mind but I felt that someone was watching over me, because when I got to the place where I was going to do wrong something moved inside of me and right there in the middle of the street I fall to my bended knees.

Now I can not understand why God choose to save me and I understand now it was His Holy Spirit hitting on me. Now to some people I might have looked foolish that day but to me that was the day that God took full control of me. I can't tell you how good it felt to know that God is always with me.

But I will tell you I was about to do wrong when somebody hit me.

THE BEST OF BOTH WORLDS

HER DIRTY
LITTLE SECRET

See I was her dirty little secret, her lover in the late hours of the night. I was her teddy bear that she spoke about to others but was never seen. For it was every night in the late hours I would fulfill her passion and weaken both her body and her knees.

Some nights I even took her to Heaven before she could count to three; see this woman had the body of a Goddess; every one of her features was formed and molded right for her from her head to her feet making her built for pure delight.

And her eyes were like stars twinkling in the late hours of the night. There upon her chest sat two of the sexiest looking breasts filled with the milk of nature. All making her slender but well-shaped body a delight to every man she meets.

But it was the passion of her love making that took a bit out of me. Each time we made love she completed me as we both brought out the wonders in each other's ecstasy but I was her dirty little secret known only to her and me.

I GIVE YOU ME

It is amazing to me that God can see something within me. That He makes the people of the world unable to see. Is it only because He created me or planted me within my father's seed and my mother's belly?

It is amazing to me that He can find a way to change the person within me and others can not see that change. Maybe it's because they refuse to see it or maybe it's that they want me to remain in the misery that man has in store for me.

It is even more amazing that He can grant me a love unlike any other love that a woman can experience or has seems. She is still quick to judge me by the other things that man has done to her and not judge me by me. Could she not see that within me, just like Adam, I was formed from the dirt of the Earth within my mother's belly, through my father's seed? And God gave me power and dominion over man and beast. He also gave me dominion over my destiny and yet the sin of loneliness had fallen upon me.

God looked into my eyes and saw this sin and for that He put me to sleep and while I was sleeping He chosen to remove a rib from my body to create what He called man's greatest dream woman. He stood you there before me and within you I found a beauty unlike anything I had ever witness or seen.

My heart broke out into a song and I found myself praising God for what He had given to me and in the mist of you standing there even the wind, the birds and the beast of the Earth rejoiced over you being given to me. For God tells us that He will not withhold any good thing from us.

THE BEST OF BOTH WORLDS

I DIDN'T ASK

Someone said a prayer today and I know God must have heard it. For I felt something move within my heart

Today somebody asked Him to give them a word
That they might use to help others see His work

Yes today somebody asked Him for just a little touch
To heal their body from sickness with His blood

Today someone asked Him to give them faith
That they might overcome the devil's way

Yes, somebody said a prayer today
And I know God must have heard it
For I felt something within my knees today

It was me that praised Him but I didn't ask the Lord for worth or fame. But I did ask Him to send me a treasure of a far more lasting kind.

I asked Him for happiness in all things great and small
I asked Him to grant me health and blessing,
For myself, my family and all

For today I am not the man I used to be
And I don't see life the same

See someone said a prayer today
And they said it for me
For it was Jesus asking his father to change my name for me

And to grant me a favor with those I might meet
And be my shepherd and I his sheep

Someone said a prayer today
And I know God must have heard it
Because tears began running down my cheeks

A. L. WATKINES

ONE
WISH

If I had one wish...
    it would not be to have a million dollars, but to have
    you close to me. It would not be to have a nice car or
    home and most of all not the money to buy all these
    worldly things.

If I had one wish...
    it would not be to be famous or play for some big
    basketball or football team but it would be to see you
    each night in my arms and in my dreams.

If I had one wish...
    understand me when I say it would not be to be
    President or some country's king it would be that you
    as the woman in my life would help me to fulfill all my
    and your hopes and dreams.

If I had one wish...
    it would not be to be seen by the world on some
    newspaper or magazine as the most handsome black
    man the world had ever seen, it would be that you
    would love and care for me as I would love and care
    for you with all the love that God has given me.

If I had one wish...
    it would not be to be seen in the movies or on TV but to
    have you love me with the same love that you have for
    yourself and the same love that God has for me and
    you.

If I had one wish...
    it would not be to have you far away from me this
    Christmas and New Year's Eve, but to pop my fingers
    like Bewitched and in a moment have you standing
    right here in front of me.

ONE
WISH

If I had one wish…
    it would not be to see you walking with some other
    black man beside you other than me, but to have you
    always close to me as my wife, my lover and my
    worldly queen.

If I had one wish …
    it would not be to have all these things rolled up into
    one and not let them be a dream.

JUST A 'THANK YOU'

Lord here it is another morning you have granted me to wake and see. Although my walk with you is not as it should be, this morning I am praying to you not in my bed but on the floor on bended knees. I want to say **Thank You** for your many blessings such as the gift of life you trusted within me; for opening door that man has closed within my face as well as those doors that I could not see.

Thank You Lord for always being by my side. **Thank You** that you're God all by yourself. Most of all **Thank You** for all that you have done in my life; for you have put bread on my table and clothes on my back.

You have made a way out of no way when there seems to be no way. You have been my protector every step of the way even when I refused to believe that there was a God. Your Angel of mercy was always by my side. **Thank You** Lord for those times when I was driving down the highway and did not know where I was going and the rain was so hard that I could not see.

Thank You for seeing something within me that I did not see within myself. For believing in me when no one else would believe. For Lord, you have been the food that I need not only when I was hunger but the food for my mind **Thank You** Lord for being there when I was a little weak in the body you were the strength to make me strong and I just want to tell you **Thank You.**

Thank You when my enemies came against me you wrapped your arms around me; when drug dealers and killers lived right next door to me you always made sure your armor was upon me. **Thank You** Lord for the times that my mother and grandmother interceded in prayer for me. **Thank You** for your words being planted within me and those late hours in the night that you spoke to me.

JUST A
'THANK YOU'

<u>Thank You</u> for always keeping a roof over my head and for my friends and family. Thank you for being an awesome God, a merciful God. <u>Thank You</u> for your grace and for teaching me to love with true love not worldly love. <u>Thank You</u> for forgiveness and showing me how to forgive others as you has forgiven me. <u>Thank You</u> for the understanding of knowing our way is not always your way and to stop trying to do things myself. So Lord I poise this morning to say **Thank you for I don't know what tomorrow might bring but for today I want to Thank you for all you have already done.**

A. L. WATKINES

OLD SCHOOL BROTHER

I am just a old school brother, private as can be and been hurt by love so much, that I was out to get the women in my life before they got me.

Now love had got so fearful in me to tell the truth I would not let anyone get close to me.

See I once wanted to be pleasing in God's eyes that was what love meant to me but there was something inside me that just loved to party in the streets. Had so many women their names sometime got the best of me so I called them all Beautiful to make it so easy on me.

Now trying to remember all my lies to each one of them, I thought that no man could beat me. But Mama always said someday those same lies will bring me to my knees.

Now I would take my paycheck on Friday and be broke by Monday but the rest of the week it all belonged to me.

Now did I tell you that I was a married sexiest womanizer for any man could see? When I was lost in my sins of life this woman stood beside me. I said that I wanted love and each day and night she tried her best to give it to me. But how could I love a woman like her when I did not love myself. She brought me the best of clothes, shoes and food to eat. I drove one of the nicest cars anyone could have on my street.

She always gave me money to help supply my needs. And when I was sick she would always pray for me.

Even though her mother did not like me and she died putting a jinx on me; her sister loved me. Because before my wife, she and I used to have a thing. Now her brother he wanted to hurt me because he could see the no good man within me.

OLD SCHOOL BROTHER

See I am an old school brother, private as can be and I thought I knew love and how to win any women off her feet. Smooth way of talking and dressing each day to be seen.

Then one day it hit me, God opened my wife eyes to see the real me. And before I knew it this old school brother was put out into the street with just the clothes on my back and the shoes on my feet.

Love can be a beautiful thing if you're not blinded by every woman you might see. If you give it a chance and love just might bring you to your knees.

A. L. WATKINES

MY DADDY

My Daddy was my Batman and I was his Robin with the whole world as our Gotham City to defeat.

We had so much fun fishing and climbing trees, playing football and watching the neighborhood girls walk down the city street.

Then one day without a word he just up and left me. Each day after school I waited for him on the front porch stairs - through rain and snow. Hoping that he would again come and we would once again do all our favorite things.

After so long, the days just seemed to pass away and days became months and months became years and still my Daddy was no where to be seen.

Now within my mind I wondered if he left because of me. Was it something I did or something I said that made him just up and leave.

Now I am all grown and there is still a strong hurt inside of me as I wonder if that same up and leave seed is planted inside of me.

For God has given me a son and he means the world to me. Yet I don't know how to love him after the day my Daddy up and left me.

Now there is that fear that one day I will up and leave for they say the apple doesn't always fall far from the tree.

THE BEST OF BOTH WORLDS

NO GREAT LOVER

I am no Romeo, no Casanova, no player
for these men I could never be

No I am no pimp, no mack or gigolo
For those kind of men are not in me.

I used to think I was a lover,
but how could I love somebody
when I didn't know how to love me

I used to think I had it going on,
but I was only fooling me.

See I had the nicest of cars,
money in the bank, nice clothes and the best shoes on my
feet but I was only impressing me.

I used to think I had done al these things for myself, for I
forgot who gave me the power to work and to stand on my
feet. I forgot who opened my eyes each morning and gave
me the power to see

I forgot who feed me when I was hungry
and watched over me when I was sleep
I forgot who held me when I was sick and weak

I forgot who told me to just believe and to put my faith and
trust in Him, most of all I forgot who carried me all those
times when I was in need. Who opened doors man had
closed before me.

No I am no Romeo, no Casanova, no player
for these kind of men are not me
And yet I must admit I am not perfect,
but I know I am not the man I used to be

A. L. WATKINES

NO GREAT LOVER

I was sitting here watching the waves as they moved over
the sea, dreaming of when you and I will be together as one
for no other woman could have made me so complete.

Next to God, for you I will stay on my knees,
keep asking God what did I do to deserve you
He told me, Son, just have faith and believe
For someone prayed for thee

Because no pimp, no mack or gigolo
can see you the way I see you.

THE BEST OF BOTH WORLDS

A TOWER OF GRAY

The beauty of her gray
Hair covering her strong round face

Her skin was coco butter
Brown which would bring a
smile to every young
and older man's with grace

And yet her body was
created like that of a
woman who could have
just stepped out of a magazine

In her younger years
She was known as the
Dance hall Queen

Every part of her walk
Moved in such a way
It was like watching
The movement of rushing waves
Over an ocean sea

Her eyes were soft but
They spoke of her love in every way

And when she would speak her
Words had meaning in such a
Powerful way

Her fingers were long like
The branches of a tree
Holding fruit as strong
Winds try to blow them away

And her legs were sexy to
The point they could turn
a man's head without a word

A. L. WATKINES

A TOWER OF GRAY

She told us of her time
Being born in slavery and
of how things used to be

She even told of those
Who broke free and got away
And those who got caught
And sold the next day

She told of how she found
A way to walk with
Dr. Martin Luther King Jr. before
He got shot down that spring day

And she told of how her
husband was taken by men
With white sheets covering their faces

She told of how she danced
with the William Brother
and sung next to Mahalia Jackson on stage

She told of how she had
Seen the lightening flash and
The thunder row and she heard
God's voice that day

She said joy will come if
You just hold out, she
Told of how her day would
Come and she will be with the Lord
With a smith upon her face
I remember the beauty of her gray hair
Covering her strong round face

TOUCH OF FORBIDDEN LOVE

A. L. WATKINES

THE FOOD STORE OF LOVE

Today my imagination has gotten the best of me.
As I laid down last night to go to sleep for some reason I woke up in 1950.

Driving an old model car with you sitting in the seat next to me, singing an old love song we were listening on the radio
With words that were touching the inner soul of us
Now when the song was done on the radio

Then came the news and it was related to me and you
For some reason they called me Clyde and your name was Bonnie.

Now they claimed that we
had just robbed **the food store of love**
And that we took it for its complete goodies
They say we stole a jar filled with **compassion**
And a can of **joy**,
A bottle of **romance**
And a box filled with **understanding mixed with exotic**

Then they say we stole a carton **made of sex**
And **a loaf of love**
A bag of **gentleness**
And **some lunch meat made from warmth**
Along with some eggs made of **happiness**
Bacon mixed with **performs**
Chips mixed with a **touch of pain**

Now they say there was **some comfort in there**
But to tell the truth I did not see it
And they say on the shelf there was **a song of peace**
Along with paper bags filled **with knowledge**
Also they say there was **meat of all kind - steaks made of ability**

THE BEST OF BOTH WORLDS

THE FOOD STORE
OF LOVE

And **pork chops made of achievement**
Hamburger made from judgment
Along with some sugar made of **disappointment**
And then there was this ham with was created from **creditableness**

And some TV dinners **made by nature high**
There was ice cream made by **history**
Don't forget that behind the counter was some **love mixes**

Well I will never forget that day for the police arrested
us right around the corner from our house

So we never got to mixed any of those ingredients
Of what the world **call worldly love**
Oh yeah before I forget

There was **some chocolate candy made from fun**
And some breathe mints made of loneliness
With some gum drops mixed with trust
And all this together was known as a relationship

A. L. WATKINES

MY NUBIAN QUEEN

See today we live more for the world and less for ourselves. To say these things, but understand I don't live my life for the world. You as a woman have pulled life back into me because you make me laugh. I enjoy the times we talk and most of all I enjoy the woman I see within you. As a woman you have opened my blinded eyes so once again I can see the one thing that I once refused.

My heart is overwhelmed that I have found myself so now when I think about loving myself, I find myself thinking about how to enjoy you. My desire is to be there for you as a friend for you have become my minister. I want to heat your soul when things seem cold. You are the spiritual song that I sing in the early part of the morning and closing as nights end.

See I want to be the instrument of peace that is a special part of you. Believe it or not you are the reason that I am here. God brings people into our life for a reason and it is more about you than me. Now if you need me I will be whatever you need for you are that light in the darkness of the night; that the world now seeks so freely and openly. And with that feeling I feel I can count on you and no matter what anyone says you're God's gift to me at the right time for me.

Forgive me because my desire is to someday live the remaining of my life with the love of my life and these kinds of feeling are new within me.

To tell the truth these feelings have really knocked me off my feet; I caught me off guard, blindsided me, and it has gotten to the point that I just got to tell somebody. I am like the blind man at the temple when Jesus opened his eyes.

THE BEST OF BOTH WORLDS

MY NUBIAN QUEEN

I just have to share what you have done in my life with other and not care what they might think we seem to fit together like a hand to a glove. In so many ways, you understand me when I say that I would have never thought that I would have found Heaven here on earth.

There were times when I thought that God would not forgive me for my wrongs, and yet in this short time you have given me what I needed the most by showing me God's favor on me by entrusting me with your friendship and your willingness to share with me your wisdom. No other woman had every offered me that before or maybe it was that I would not let it come into my life.

In my mind you are worth going to the alter for in prayer we seem to communicate so well and I want to learn to love you from my side of life and how to light the fire and wisdom inside of you, understand this is not a game take this down within your soul.

A. L. WATKINES

THIS WOMAN I MEET

I met this woman and she invaded my privacy and before I knew it she way right through me, even the things I refuse to let other people see, it was as if it could have been something wrong within in or maybe it was that I could not have respected her it was as if God created her for me, but if so, why did it take Him so long to send her to me, like I said, this woman invaded my privacy to the point I wanted to know all about her from the crown of her head to the toe's upon her feet, I even wanted to know where certain spots were that would make her react to me in an erotic way, I wanted to know where she wanted my fingers to run when I touched her body of held her in my arms. I wanted to know the sign and if she was looking for a man or just for a friend, see, I wanted to know her buried secrets and where was her hidden treasure. I wanted her to tell me her fantasies, and if we could steal way one night, for her body always seems to smell like African violets with just the right scent of candy apple, like I said this woman she invaded my privacy, see she made me undress her with my eyes and she relieved all my fears, she taught me how and gave me a reason to love again and she made me desire to be a better man, and to put away my past, she reminded me of a smooth jazz solo coming to take me away from the things of this world by letting me melt into the simplistic chocolate of her skin to the point that I wanted to blend in so perfectly see I needed to be needed and be everything she required of me to be submissive to her I wanted to drown in her like water she was the perfect key on a baby grand.

THE BEST OF BOTH WORLDS

LATE HOURS IN THE NIGHT

Many late hours in the night I could hear her praying and most of the time I will admit it was for me. See there was no greater sinner within my household then me. The bad thing about it was that she knew that God had a calling on me. See He had gave me that kind of voice to touch the heart of those who would not believe but how could I touch their heart when within side of me I did not believe; He gave me wisdom and knowledge that I refused to receive willingly.

But when I learned how to use it I used them to lie and deceive to benefit me, and then for some reason He gave me understanding. Told me all that I had to do was ask Him and He would give me the understanding to all things that I needed clear to me but I took that understanding and used it as a gift, To see into the future of those who would pay good money to me. Now I was never one to ask Him for patience. Always wanted everything right away for me a nice home and a lot of money was not the things for me. I was the kind of man that was never into material things, found myself never using drugs, drinking alcohol - all this was not for me. Just like David, give me a finely built woman and you have found the weakness within me.

Always wanted friends for that I would lie, steal and cheat but for some reason I wanted people to like me. Never knew it was that I did not like myself that made me seek out friends to complete me. Yes there were many late hours in the night I could hear her praying for my soul and most of the time it was for me. I asked myself sometime now why it is that God chose to love me when I had a brother who was willing to do His will at the drop of a hat. Many times an answer I did not receive, many nights she would come and anointed my head when she thought that I was asleep and I could hear her cursing that devil within me even until the day that God took her home within her sleep she still prayed for me.

A. L. WATKINES

IT'S SO EASY
TO LOVE YOU

It's so easy to love you because in my heart and my mind I believe God created you just for me. I refuse to let the Devil play mind games with me because you are well worth the wait.

It's so easy to love you because no matter what wall, foolishness or thought's the Devil place in my mind or face. No matter what storm, rain or torment pass relationships has put me through. I find it so easy to love you.

It's so easy to love you because you're wonderful in so many different ways!

It's so easy to love you because I can look at your photo and a smile comes upon my face and I find myself enjoying the moment as if you were my favorite glass.

It's so easy to love you because when I look at you my heart wants to take you to places you have never been. Show the world what God has chosen for me. The tears that might flow from my face is my desire to teach you how to love me; how to be loved by a real man and not a boy in a man's body.

It's so easy to love you because your voice tells me you're looking for love. Yet your mind questions the love you have found with me and within yourself.

It's so easy love you because I believe if I have never believed anything before you will stand beside your man not in front or in back of him.

It's so easy to love you because in you I find a reason to want to keep you safely within my arms. If that won't do I will try something new. Understand it's so easy to love you because within my mind I have touched you, held you and kissed you a hundred times.

THE BEST OF BOTH WORLDS

IT'S SO EASY
TO LOVE YOU

It's so easy to love you because within you I see the kind of woman I have raised my daughters to be. That makes it easy to love you because you're blessed with a beauty and a body that keeps me on bended knees.

It's so easy to love you because you bring out a man that was so hidden inside of me; a man that I once refused to be. You are my Princess, my Cinderella and in my hand I hold the shoe that will make you completely mines.

Like I said it's so **easy to love you** because when I say that you
are the air that I breathe

Some say that it is better to have loved and lost it
But I say it is better to have not loved at all

That is why **it's so easy to love you**.............

A. L. WATKINES

HOW COULD GOD MAKE HER?

How could God make someone so beautiful and not keep her for himself? How can he make her an Angel and not give her wings but place her here upon Earth for man to witness and see? How can He entrust someone so special and place her in the hands of someone like me? Someone who never knew love and never knew it the way He has shown love to me after all these times. I have been blind and I never knew how to love me, sometimes there are no words to express what He touched within me and changed the old man that was once inside of me, now the world don't believe that I am me.

How could God make someone so beautiful and not keep her for himself for He has touched her in all the right ways that man would see love? Yet He formed her to be a help mate unto man not his sexual dream. He gave her wisdom to not think as a man would think. The knowledge to encourage man to be all that God would have him to be and all that he is called to be.

Then He blessed her with eyes to see far beyond the forest from the trees. He enriched her with an understanding of what a man help mate would need. He gave her the power to be as beautiful as a rose opening its petal at the first sight of spring. In some ways He gave her the power to be a companion to those in need of a blessing the way that Adam needed Eve.

How could God make someone so beautiful and not keep her for himself? He installed within her a will to lead just as He gave Moses the power to lead his people to be free. Then He placed in her heart this thing they call love that could help her overcome her greatest enemies. He gave her also the overwhelming gift it's called practices to deal with man His first creation after making the world complete.

THE BEST OF BOTH WORLDS

LOVING AND BEING IN LOVE

Loving and being in love with someone like you have helped me to understand what I have been missing. They say that love is making it through the hard times even when everything that you do seem to turn out wrong but you still have each others back.

Love is not sweating the small things that might come your way but learning to turn them over to the Lord. Leaving them with Him and it knows without a doubt within your mind that you have each other along with God by your side.

Love is compromising and juggling responsibilities and seeing through to the other persons' heart of what really matters to them and to each others not just to you.

Love is finding a way throughout your day to have some alone time with each other even if it is just a phone call or a quickie at home when so many other things seem to get in the way of your time alone at home.

Love is learning and teaching each other how to love one another without holding back what it is that you want and what it is that you have to give. Yet it is doing the simplest things that will make each other happy or feel special; like buying roses for no reason or dinner out at their favorite place to eat. Maybe even cooking dinner time after time, whether you know it or not.

Love is being willing to share with each other without fear of hurting each other feelings, and love is being willing to share your life together with each other not looking for flakes. But looking for understanding. Love is knowing that your both is willing to give your best with out holding back even when it feel like you have nothing left to give.

A. L. WATKINES

LOVING AND BEING IN LOVE

Love is seeing something within each other that no other person has seen. Most of all love trusts each other through the good times and well as the bad even when the bad out weight the good. Love is listen to each other as well as hearing each other's voice when their are no where around. It is having someone to lean on and never feeling lost in the relationship, and it is ever being lonely.

Love is a slip of some cold wine while sitting in each others' arms; it is being each other companions. Love is finding yours and hers favorite love song.

Lastly love loves someone and being loved in returned to the point everyday you just want to do a little more to show that person your love for them. **Love is just one word but it says it all!**

MADE IN HIS IMAGE

He said that I was made in His image. Then why is there so much wrong within me? Was it given to me by my Earthly Father or was it from Adam's seed. For when I seek to do good there seems to be no good within me. And sometimes when I kneel down to pray, it seems as if God sometime doesn't hear me.

But His word says 'blessed is the man that walk not in the counsel of the ungodly nor stands in the way of sinners nor sits in the seat of scornful, for He is a delight in the law of God and He shall be like a tree planted by the rivers of water if He has the faith to believe'.

For He said that I am made in His image then why is there so much wrong within me? Was it given to me by my Earthly Father or was it from Adam's seed? For God told me I could have anything that I desire. Then somebody tell me why these bills are getting the best of me, my kids need shoes and I need food within this house to eat. The other day my dog bit me, because he too just like the rest of us is hungry. My landlord came over the other day for his rent and I pretended like I was asleep. I tell you it seems as if God has turned His back on me and yet He said I was made in His image. Then why is there so much wrong within me? Again was it given to me by my Earthly Father or was it from Adam's seed?

He says that I am healed from His stripes, but the doctor told me I have cancer and it's eating up the insides of me. So I called on God to remove this cancer from within me. See people, others told me He had done it for them then why can't He do it for me. But in the mean time my family is making burial plans for me just in case His stripes don't get to help me.

MADE IN HIS IMAGE

He says that I am made in His image then why is there so much wrong within me? Was it given to me by my Earthly Father or was it from Adam's seed? Now His word tells me I can defeat my enemies then why do these people at work seem it get the best of me? Not a day goes by that I don't have to fall on bended knees or hold back my hands to keep from knocking someone off their feet but I know that He is watching over me.

For I am made in His image, He created me and it seem like every morning He gives the gift of life. And no matter how much I doubt He always give me my needs.

For only He knows what is best for me, now when sickness hits my body His word is what heals me and He gives me the power to defeat my enemies. And the wrong that is within me He tells me to turn it over to Him and He will remove it from me if I have the faith and just believe.

For I am made in His image and God is not a man to lie.

THE BEST OF BOTH WORLDS

A RAINDROP

I thought I felt a raindrop fall upon me but when I looked up toward Heaven. The sky was clear as could be and as blue as an ocean and as I turned away, I thought I heard a voice call out to me. But when I looked around nobody did I see; it was then that I thought that I felt somebody arms around about me. When I touched myself on the side I felt only me, so I walked a little further and it was as if someone was walking with me. I turned and looked to both sides of me and all I could see was the ocean, forest and trees.

It was then that I came to a bench below an old oak tree and I found myself sitting under it. Wondering if something had come over me as the ray of the sun seemed to blind me. When I opened my eyes standing before me was this Angel with two wings.

She was a beautiful Black queen with skin that looked like it was made from the sweetest of honey just taken from the hive of the Queen Bee. Now upon her was this well shaped body, slim and yet petite. With long black hair down her back and eyes as black as pearls found within the deepest of an ocean sea. There upon her face sat two of the most tempting lips that I had once seen within my dreams and the roundness of her face made everything else seemed so complete. Her hips seemed to move like thunder as she walked towards me and the perfume smell coming from her body was like that of a gentle wind blowing between two trees.

The sound of her gentle voice brought out something unknown within me. When she touched me I felt my heart crying as it seemed to miss every other beat. So I closed my eyes hoping to open them again and find this all to be only a dream. But just right there it begin to rain long rivers of water upon me.

A. L. WATKINES

A TEARDROP OF LOVE FOR YOU

My God woman when I look at you and see the beauty that you give out as a woman there is more than enough for the eyes to see. There is a beauty within you that lies far beyond any joy that a man could receive. For within you there is a touch of essence that seems to have found a way to warm a corner within my heart and soul.

There is this need to want to fulfill your desires and dreams of what a relationship should be. You are like the nature of a soft wind blowing between two trees that must be taken slowly with in by a man. You must understand that I am not only seeking your soul, it is your heart that I am looking for and nothing else would bring out the inter man within me.

Sometimes I wonder if there is love within you and if there is a need for a man. Tell me are you a self made woman that feels you can do it alone? For was it not God who gave unto Adam a woman and He called her Eve. For she was the most beautiful of all creatures upon the Earth.

Now each night within my mind I lie on my sheets upon my bed and place my favorite pillow by your gentle head. As I lay back I can hear your voice whispering within my ear and I see myself loving you and getting to know you. Shall I walk away from this degree of love and wanting to release all my inner love to you? Yet I only want to give you my best. See I want nothing more then a commitment of your heart. For the color of my skin does not change the man within me.

So I am caught up in this love thing with someone that I don't know as the world say that I should. For it is my belief, that you're who God would have for me but once again the Devil seeks to steal my joy of finding you.

He have released this loneliness from me by deceiving me into believing that love has no room for me within a woman's heart, for the world can be so cruel and so mean.

THE BEST OF BOTH WORLDS

A TEARDROP OF
LOVE FOR YOU

Shall I walk around with my feeling within my hands? Today I felt a tear run down my cheek as I thought of me and you becoming one. I must admit the feeling was good because it came from within me and from knowing God.

A. L. WATKINES

COMFORT OF
A WOMAN

It is as if it was the last game of the season and I was playing. The ball was in my hand, as I went up to make the winning shot I dropped the ball and my team loss.

Sometime it's so hard to get you to understand me and to bring you back to the woman I fell in love with.

It seems as if the things that are in your mind or on your mind out weigh the love you share or once shared with me.

When I ask you about them you tell me it's nothing - knowing that you have become apart of me and when something is wrong with you there is something wrong with me. Yet I want to feel that I can trust you with my life and yet you don't trust me with what's on your mind good or bad.

See when I think of you and I, I know within my heart there will be that blessed day. When in my mind I can sit back and think of all that I had to go through in order for God to give me a woman like you. You are so beautiful and so gifted and at times it's hard to believe that you are apart of me.

See sometime ago I used to think that I was God's gift to women but here I am today thanking God for his gift of women to me. I won't complain because what we have between us is more than I had ever dreamed of. I am so close to someone without ever touching them or seeing them face to face; just know God thought enough of me to not turn his back on me when it comes to what I had asked him for the woman in my life to be.

In this time frame you have given me an extraordinary love. If you only knew what that mean and yet I don't want you to feel that I am trying to put chains on you.

COMFORT OF A WOMAN

Thank you for giving me your shoulder to lean on and yet sometimes cry on without knowing that I was crying. See sometimes even the strongest of men have to cry.

Thank you for knowing how to put a smile on my face even though you could not see it there. Know that it felt so warm inside of me because you smiled back. Yet those times when I was the doctor, listened to everyone's problems daily and needed lifting up just know that hearing your voice when you called at the right moment. At the right time sparked peace throughout me.

Only if you could have seen the tears that rushed down my face, sometimes I must admit you take my breathe away and sometimes you brought out that island man within me that made me so mad because God made me wait to receive the best thing that had come to me....the comfort of you as a woman.

There were moments when you make me speechless. Those times are when I looked in your eyes within your picture and I think back to that first day I laid eyes on you. I told myself that Heaven had opened its gates and gave me one of his Angels.

I thank God for you because besides Him no one else can make me feel the way that I do towards you. Understand for there is nothing like the comfort of a woman beside a man.

A. L. WATKINES

A TOUCH OF UNSEEN BEAUTY

They say she had no ideal how beautiful she was. For it seemed as if others could see what she could not see within him. For so many times in her younger years, she had been told that she was ugly by others who were just being mean.

And yet in her mind for sometime this was all that she believed. So when she would look in her bedroom mirror, she could not see her beautiful brown rose colored skin, her black pearl eyes and her sensual lustful lips nor her thunderous way of walking into a room. She could

She could not see the overwhelming form of her body. The firmness of her long petite legs with her fully shaped neither breasts nor the way her neck held up her head.

Even though none of these things could be seen by her, but with in her mind she continued to hope for a relationship and dreams of love because she had never known love.

For she had never been touched by a man other then her father when he held her to tell her of his love for her as a father. Her lips had never felt the warmth of a man lips against hers and she had never looked into a man eyes and seen love in a heat of passion. For her voice seems to cry out for these things. She had never smelled the scent of a man's body after a shower - for it had always been her own body scent that she embraced.

That at times seems to cause her to have a sexual awakening many times within her mind. For it seems as if she had a beauty unseen by her.

DEFINITION OF A REAL MAN

The definition of a real man is the understanding of a woman. A real man is one who has learned to love himself and who knows the good within himself.

He is a man who is confident in whom he is and knows what he has in a good woman before it is gone!

He is a man who is not afraid to pray but also is not afraid to cry. A real man is a man who will give himself as a living sacrifice to not only God but to the woman and children within his life. A real man will seeks the advice of God before seeking the advice of man. A real man knows that his life is not his own but with God he can do all things.

A real man will always see a beauty within the woman in his life that no other man has seen within her.

A real man is very careful of his words and the way that he speaks them. A real man will seek to know his woman needs without her having to inform him for he will always do these special things to show that he cares. Most of all a real man will seek to learn the ways of his woman and how to love her. He will walk besides her not in front of her; he will love her as he loves his mother and the church.

A real man will never abuse a woman, with his hands or words, because he will always remember that he will reap what he sow. He will always take the time out to talk to his woman because understanding and communication is the most important factors within a relationship. A real man will not listen to what others say about his woman but judge her for what he sees within her.

For these are the things that define the definition of a real man. See a real man will provide for his woman as well as his kids. He opens doors that no other man has opened within her life. He will not look down or talk down to her but with each day he will seek ways to build her up.

A. L. WATKINES

A BLACK MAN'S LOVE

A Black man's love that his woman understands that he is not perfect and never will be

A Black man's love that no matter what might come their way she will stay by his side through thick and thin but she will not take any mess

A Black man's love that he will never love her the same as any other woman of his past

A Black man's love that he might forget at times to tell her how beautiful she is but hoping she will already know that she is

A Black man's love that they will always have disagreements and that he/she might walk out and leave but that he/she will always return back to their home

A Black man's love that he can trust her to go out with her unmarried friends but still remember she got a man at home and the same goes for him

A Black man's love that he will never treat her as less then the woman God made her to be and not more then she presents herself to be

A Black man's love her to be his most intoxicated drink that he is unable to put down daily

A Black man's love that they both are not blind to the beauty that they
both see around them but not to touch

A Black man's love that ain't no mountain high enough or no valley low
enough that they can not communicated with each other about anything

THE BEST OF BOTH WORLDS

A BLACK MAN'S LOVE

A Black man's love that he does not always have to have a reason to buy her roses and other material things to prove his love

A Black man's love that they both have an understanding when understanding is needed

A Black man's love that he or she shall not judge a book by its cover because you never know what the pages might read like inside

A Black man's love that he is a stallion in bed when it comes to making love to her and him don't need any medical help

A Black man's love when to eliminate all obstacles that might hinder their relationship and yet it is never having to sing the blues

A Black man's love she deserve the best that he has to give and the best that he can be because he's a man

A Black man's love that he is able to always make her feel special in every way as a woman

A. L. WATKINES

STARTING MY DAY WITH YOU

Today I started my day with you, so I decided to….

Let nothing come between us unless it is God and to let nothing make each other sad with the other because we now hold each other within our heart. Let nothing come between us that we can not talk about and let nothing come between us to make us lose what we have found within each other.

So let nothing come between us for last night I prayed that I as a man would never let my worldly man do anything wrong to cost you hurt and pain nor to make you want to leave me. For it is hard living alone and being alone; understand I think of you daily you have become life to me. Yet I will always and clearly do my best to love and honor you for the woman that I see within you.

And if given the chance I will love you with all I have within me and through all the things that we as a couple will be forced to see. So just wait and give me a chance to show you that my love and understanding is well worthy of your love.

For I will be there with you in your sickness, your private doctor I will examine you from your head to your feet. I will be there in your happiness and in your health. I will be the man that you need me to be and if it is God's will I will be there in your riches and wealth. Unlike any other man all these things I promise to give to you if you will receive and believe in me as I have learned to believe in you. For it will be then that I can wake up in the morning knowing within my heart and mind that **I am starting my day with loving you.**

THE BEST OF BOTH WORLDS

ROMEO & JULIET

Like Romeo and Juliet I thought our love would surpass the test of time to me you were my favorite glass of wine on a hot day in the summer time you were my Rose in a garden of weeds.

Each morning when you would awaken, I would wait to see the sun rise within you for no one else could hold a candle next to the woman I saw within you. Inside your garden I felt so safe, I felt a joy inside my heart like never before and a God fearing love that was just for me.

But how can a man love when he doesn't know real love? How can he understand when no one has taught him how to understand love? How can he not fear love when the fear of being hurt by love is all that he has known?

How could I not enjoy the beauty that I saw within you? How could I not enjoy when you held my hand or looked into my eyes and called me your man? How could I not understand the touch of your lips upon mine or the gentleness of your voice? Or the way you made me feel in your garden?

But just like so many other men I was blinded by my old ways; by not putting my trust in God but by putting my trust in me.

Why did I let my feeling get the best of me? Why could I not see the forest from the trees or that my friends did not want you as apart of me? How could I let the best gift of God leave me?

Here I stand in your garden just as Romeo without his Juliet...

A. L. WATKINES

YOU GOT ME ALL WRONG

Now I can begin this with lies. But there are times when you can't always tell the truth. I looked at your photo today and in you I saw the woman of my dreams.

But tell me why when I am with you, you pass judgment on me? Tell me what is within me that you see is wrong? Why can you look at me and see the man that God made me to be and not the man the world would have me to be? Or do you look at me and see every other man that you had in your past life?

Do you look at the words I write as being full of lies and deceit? Or is it that you can't believe a man can see you for the woman you are and not some one to supply his sex needs?

Can you not believe that a man can see you for the woman God created you to be? For do you think that you have something in you or on you that he cannot find in another woman that he might seek?

For you got me all wrong and you need to take another look at me. Could it be the words I say that made you feel like the woman you need to be but because you distance yourself from me and you refuses to believe in me?

Or just maybe its' been so long that the thought of a real man has put fear within you. Could it be that you are really not looking for anyone and this is a game you are playing? Just to pass time with ease.

Tell me what makes you any better than me? I am sorry if it is a thug or a player that you are seeking or even a drug dealer that could have the power to bring you to your knees. All of which I am not and will never be.

Tell me I would like to know what it is that you see so wrong within me could it possibly be that I have a college degree.

ONE STEP
CLOSER

I have seen you before many times in my dreams but never before have I thought that God would show this kind of favor on me. Understand my walk with HIM is not as it should be. For I have turned my back on Him; but He has never turned His back on me. It's just like God knows it He still saw some good within me.

See just like Adam for so long I've been in this garden hoping to someday find my Eve. This rib of mines is getting the best of me, the bible say that man should not be alone so what's going on with me. Never thought that you would be the woman of my dreams but I must say that day I first laid eyes on you something strange came over me and unlike any other woman you seem to connect with me. For that reason you deserve a chance at getting to know the man within me. See it's not easy to get next to me, you opened my eyes to something I refuse to see and that maybe I could love again without the fear of love playing its game on me. Now I understand that you're only human and that the miracle that I am seeking is within me and yet I have never witness anything that I can compare to the beauty that I see when you look at me.

For you're my touch of hot chocolate surrounded by sweet white cream with cherries for lips and eyes that remind me of looking into an ocean sea. For your body has been blessed by God from the crown of your head to your toes.

I would be wrong not to admit as a man it does something within me, the way your hips move you have the power to bring even the strongest man to his knees to make the weak man seek strength.

A. L. WATKINES

ONE STEP CLOSER

Look at what man has done with just one seed, planted it within your mother and what a beauty he has created with that seed the beauty of your rich colored hair makes the shape of your tender face look so complete, and the gentleness of your voice is like of that of a baby when he or she is first learning to speak. You have knowledge and wisdom, understanding and a beauty that is unseen and for that I know that God is wonderful for truly He loves me and for that I would stand and tell the world He has given me my own private Angel without wings.

JUST A LITTLE BIT OF LOVE

Tonight my beloved as you walked into the room soft and smooth; I never thought this kind of feeling would happen to me again.

See only the love that I felt for God had even moved through my veins and bones to make me so weak. Yet every time I think of you, something seems to tango within me and it feels so good.

This feeling has made me love the way you wear your hair; the way it fits your face so completely.

Now I know that in the past you have been mislead by the things other men might have said to you, even promises they have made. It hurts me to know that they could not see the woman that I see within you or maybe it was that they didn't want to see you for the woman that I see.

See I love when you walk, the way your hips and thighs move like thunder across the night sky. I love the look of love in your eyes. I even love the way that you carry yourself as a woman of color. Most of all I love your motherly instincts.

Tell me has it every occurred to you that I like you for who you are; you are like a wine 'you get better with time'. I like the smell of perfume upon your body and the way you listen and understand the man in me.

Now some people might think that I want you or like you for just one thing but they can't see that you are my destiny and my queen when we grow old and gray.

A. L. WATKINES

JUST A LITTLE
BIT OF LOVE

They can't see that even if we are not always lovers we will always be friends and you will never want for anything. For you my beloved, are sexy cool, my jazzy little lady, and it is up to us to have more faith then desire.

For some things are just meant to be and it's not wrong to love from the heart.

REBIRTH

A. L. WATKINES

MANIFESTATION OF GOD

My beloved Brothers and Sisters in Christ Jesus -

I need you to be steadfast and just hold on a little longer. For I saw the manifestation of God and I witness the Gates of Heaven opened. I saw the Son of God and He spoke unto me. I was afraid because I was naked in sin therefore I ran and hide behind a tree.

For within my mind I knew that I was unworthy of God's Son talking to me. He asked unto me, "Why do you refuse to believe? For my words say come unto me and lay your burden at my feet." I cried out, "Lord have mercy on me". He said "Unto me I come to give you life more abundantly". At that very moment I felled unto my knees feeling His love for me move through the leaves of the trees behind me. Then he disappeared right before me.

Now it was not soon after that as I was standing by the ocean that again I saw the manifestation of God. Again I witness the Gates of Heaven opened. This time I saw the Apostle John and he spoke unto me. Just as I did with the Son of God I was asked in sin; so I ran and hide behind a tree.

But with a demanding voice I heard him say unto me, "Everything that happens unto me that was good". I said that the Lord did it and everything that happens unto that was bad I said the Devil lead me to it. I even ask the Son of God if he was the one to come or was there another because doubt had come over me.

I just want to tell you that God is faithful and will supply all your needs and just like He appeared he can disappear right before your eyes.

THE BEST OF BOTH WORLDS

MANIFESTATION OF GOD

Now I begin to rub my eyes hoping this was all a dream. When again I saw the manifestation of God and the Gates of Heaven opened, I saw King David and he spoken unto me. King David said, "Be not afraid, repent, have faith and believe". This time unlike the other times I did not run nor hide behind a tree for I was not naked in sin before his eyes.

I was not blinded to the point I could not see and it was right then that I fall before the Gates of Heaven raising my hands above me unto the one that gave life unto me. I witness God hands come down to touch me and the Holy Ghost filled me to the point that my spirit felt free.

Again I saw the manifestation of God but this time it felled upon me and the Gates of Heaven opened and I witnessed the Angels of Heaven rejoicing because God had delivered me; making me born again not of a corruptible seed but of a incorruptible way the word of God which liveth and abideth within me.

A. L. WATKINES

HIS COMING

Jesus must to have known......
> That we, as His people, would find it hard sometime to believe in HIS love. With the way things sometime seems and yet He had to know that there would times when we would challenge His word when we, as man, have very little faith and very little belief.

Jesus must have known....
> That it's not easy to turn away from sin.
> When it's sin that we face seven days a week.
> And He had to know that not all would be willing and ready for His day of return.

Jesus must have known....
> That in order for us to live right we had to be Baptist in his blood in order to be washed of our sins and set free.

Yes Jesus must have known...
> That our fight would be within ourselves and that we as His children must defeat the Devil and not let His kingdom are at hand.

Jesus must have known....
> That man would use His name to deceive others into believing what they believe. And He had to know that they would misuse His words to fit their needs.

Jesus must have known....
> We as His people would be loss as sheep in today's wildness with only the comforted to lead. He had to know that only some could heal the sick, feed the hunger and supply other people's needs.

> Then can someone tell me just why we choose to not open the Bible and receive that He is returning.

I MADE IT THROUGH

I tell you the truth I did not think it would happen to me but I made it through.
Now I don't understand how I woke up this morning. I will admit the body is weak maybe because I got too much sleep.

But just like the mailman I know I had to get up and do my thing. See I went to bed early last night, got more sleep then I needed, but now I know what it was that made me so sleepy now I understand it was the pain pill I took that had me weak. So I said my prayers this morning all the while hoping someone was praying for me.

For tonight I won't go to bed so early - that way I will get just the right amount of sleep. Today I made it hoping there will be no drama that should come my way. Although the weather is bad outside; today is going to be a good day.

See I am going to walk into work with a smile upon my face cause the Lord chose to wake me up this morning. So today is going to be a great day because I made it through. Many laid down last night that did not wake to see this day!

A. L. WATKINES

I TOUCHED THE FACE OF GOD TODAY

Today I touched the face of God. As I kneeled down upon my knees to pray; I looked into his eyes and I saw His favor with me. I refuse to ask the question why because so many times I had turned my back on him. Refusing to believe but was it because someone had prayed for me; was it all those times that my grandmother and mother went down on their knees or maybe it my pastor who prayed for me. See it could have even been the mother of the church, I don't know but why me.

I looked upon his skin and saw the man in him that He had chosen for me to be. Hey I was doing my thing, parties, running the streets, women and money that had a hold on me, did have time for God, hell when I prayed He did not even answer me but as I witness tears run down His and upon His cheeks and felt His love for me as a new spirit came rushing over me. I told him Lord I am not ready for this, let go of me because I touched His hair and I felt a new strength move within me. It was as if He was giving back to me what the devil had taken from me. As I watched the movement of his lips, and the words that He spoke breathe life and wisdom into me.

He put forth His hands and I could see where the nail had been placed within them so coldly. I felt all my sins being removed from me so I touched His ears so that I might hear Him when He speaks to me whether in the early morning or late at night when I am asleep. It was then that the smile upon His face showed His understanding for me and His willingness to walk with me.

I TOUCHED THE FACE OF GOD TODAY

I then looked upon His shoulder where so many times He had carried me through the rain, the storm over land and sea, upon His shoulder He help me to defeat my enemies it was then that He closed His eyes and begin to talk to His Father for me and I do believe He asked Him to keep me in His mercy and grace. Around me then like a puff of smoke His face disappeared before me, but see I touched the face of God today as I knelled down on my knees to pray and His face will forever remain within my face because He is within me.

A. L. WATKINES

IT'S NOT
TOO LATE

I've heard many men of God who could preach but not many of them God has given the power to move the inner man within me. For so many years of my life God had had a calling on me and yet many times He should have just let me be. But He kept His arms around me because He saw something within me that I refused to see. Most of my life I refused to believe that He would even hear me when I would pray or speak and yet when I poured out my needs to Him it seemed as if He turned His back on me. When I thought that it was all done He was right on time with my needs.

Never before had I've been hungry and He not put bread on my table to eat. And those times when it seems like my enemies would get the best of me He would step right in and save the night for me. Then there was those times when I was sick and could not get out of bed and I said by His stripes I am now healed.

Something moved within me and before I knew it I was on my feet; I recalled those times when someone prayed for me, they did not have to do it but they saw that special something within me and now when I look back at what He has done for me, I realize now that along time ago I should have been on bended knees.

But this man that I am speaking of has never laid eyes on me yet the power of His ministering has moved the inner man so much within me. Not only has He made me want to run to the alter but in so many ways He has brought the alter to me. He spoke to me like Jesus spoke to His people when He was on top of the hill and He touched me like Dr. Martin Luther King did when he told of his dream. I have listened to what he says that God has brought him through and his words remind me of some of the areas in my life that God has brought me through. I have always heard people say that when you have been through something, someone has been through it before you and maybe harder then you.

THE BEST OF BOTH WORLDS

GRANT ME

I know, Lord, this might be hard for you to believe coming from me, a man who never had the time to get down on bended knees. And when there was time it was only to ask for my needs. Forgetting those that are around me even my family but would you please, Lord, grant me the serenity to accept the things I can not change on my own about me. See I am tired of trying to do it myself. I need your help for when there come those times when I really just want to be me or when I forget that you're the one who supply all my needs.

And look Lord if it's not asking too much would you give me some courage like you gave to the Samson, John, and Peter? I do believe in changing the things around about me that seem to hold me back and has me doing worldly things. It just won't let me be free and they seem to keep me from becoming the man that you would have me to be or maybe it's because I refuse to accept the changes you have for me.

I know this is not too much for me to ask of Thee but please would you give me the wisdom of David and Paul to hide the anger within me; that might come up when someone around me get the best of me. Help me to be careful of the toes that I might step on; see I have some big feet. Can you find a way to bind my tongue so the words that I might speak, and if they are not your words make me stumble in my speech? For there's time Lord when I don't think before I speak and sometime my mouth can get me in trouble so quickly.

Lord grant me the understanding that Solomon had as to why so many people dislike the man they see within me. Or is it that I should look in the mirror and take a better look at myself or maybe I should try to see what you see within me. Lord in my prayers I have prayed for my enemies, I have forgave them of the wrong in which they have done to me. when I look at their face that wrong jumps right in front of me but I hold my peace, and I understand that is not the way that you have forgave me.

GRANT ME

Lord please guide my feet for sometimes they get too heavy while I am on the road driving down the street. Please make me aware of what I am doing don't need any police to stop me. See I understand it takes 42 muscles to make a frown and 58 muscles to make a smile it seem as if it better to smile, so Lord please grant me the serenity to love you as you love me.

THE BEST OF BOTH WORLDS

A BATTLE FOR THE LORD

As a warrior sit in his overstuffed favorite chair, against the living room wall. His television played the old westerns of yesterday, Gunsmoke, and the list goes on. All the while the sweet smell of fried chicken and mashed potatoes are coming from the kitchen touching his nose.

He remembered the curses he held back with smiles that sometime cracked his soul and broke his pride when it came to fighting in wars. He remembered each day that he had to put on his overalls for work and he would then put on his Godly armor over that with a smile.

He would become a diplomatic general on what was his Earthly battleground. Now he would sit back in his favorite chair and look back over his life thinking about the things he had done and the places he had been and just where God had brought him from.

He would ask God why he had to put up such a good fight to do His will and yet his battles are not yet still won? For the warrior now understand that being misunderstood is a man's way of life.

That he can win the battle but he can never win the wars because when one war passes another one is waiting to begin. So he sat quietly in his chair hoping to hear his past warrior spirit become his children and grandchildren's battle cry someday before he is taken home to be with the Lord.

A. L. WATKINES

MY PRAYER FOR YOU

Today Lord

If you never do anything else for me; you have already done enough with this woman you have sent before me. Lord look into the heart of this woman with whom I feel that you have blessed me to have eyes to see. Search within her heart and see if she is worthy of the love that you have placed within me. See if she is real with the feelings that she expressed so freely to me. Or are her words just that words and false dreams or Lord is it a game she is seeking within me.

Lord let her see that all her past mistakes with other men she will not see or find within me. Unless she is seeking a reason not to be with me, let me be a new fresh breath of air that she breathes. Not taking my feelings as a sign of weakness. Help her to understand that I see her for the woman that you have made and created her to be a gift touched by a work of art taken from man's ribs while he was asleep.

Open her heart to receive the love you have placed within me and have entrusted me to share with her. Teach her, Lord, to trust me until I give her a reason to not believe. Touch her lips so that they will thirst for me as I thirst for her and open her mind so she will be willing to give my love a try.

Let her understand that I am what she need to carry her through the good and the bad for it is now her season to receive. Please Lord don't let it be just my imagination running away with me.

MY PRAYER FOR YOU

Lord is it possible to give her what she needs; is it possible to walk with her and not in front of her. Because I am a man and is it possible that one of us can talk and the other can listen without either getting mad. Lord give her the power to not be quick to judge me by her walk with other men. Yet let her be willing to forgive me for the mistakes I might make along the way in our relationship.

Lord bless her to always remain a woman within my eyes. Let her know next to you my shoulder she can always lean on. Lord if you never do anything else for me you has already done enough with whom you have placed before me.

A. L. WATKINES

ONE OF GOD'S CHOSEN MEN

All he ever wanted was one shining moment to do Gods' work. One shining moment to earn his wings in Heaven as one of God's chosen men. So he told himself he was not just another black man for within him God had planted His word and had given it to him to share throughout the land.

But no one was willing to receive it see all he ever wanted was to save lost souls and share what as a child he had been told. All he every wanted was one shining moment to do Gods' work. For he knew that Gods' time was at hand; for he was not just some Black man sitting back taking what came down from the mouth of man. For he stood up against those who came to him with hate, racism and he told them of Gods' promise to man.

Unlike many other Black men he had the courage to stand and to hold firm to his beliefs and not just be another Black man. Even in the constant of threats, even when his brothers and sisters in Christ would not help him take a stand. Not even while the Ku Klux Klan fire bombed his home and farmland he put it all in Gods' hands.

With tears in his eyes he told the world he was God's chosen men. He said with Gods' word he would continue to make a stand. "For I will fight the good fight" he said and "carry the cross with my hands and I will preach His word like that of a God fearing man".

It was his quick action to confront intolerance, injustice and hate that placed a gun in someone hands. Just like so many others they shot down this God fearing man. And when all the investigation was done it was then that the police learned that his shooter was a Black man.

For he was not just another black man sitting back taking what came from the mouth of man. For all he ever wanted was one shining moment to do Gods' work and make a stand. One shining moment to be one of God's chosen men.

THE BEST OF BOTH WORLDS

PRECIOUS LORD

Precious Lord please takes my hand. For only you know me better then me.

Lead me on as you walk besides me during the good and bad times that face me.

Help me stand in case I slip and fall, for Lord I am tired and at times my back seemed against the wall I feel real weak and worn.

For my heart seem to rejoice when I think of where you have brought me for my body is not like it used to be.

but through the storms and the nights you can always find me on bended knees asking you to lead me to your light and when my way grows drearier I read your word to help me continue holding on.

My only request is that you linger near me because at times my enemies seems to get the best of me or when my life seems almost gone and the Devil sends his best henchmen to make me feel alone

Tell me will you hear my cries and hear my calls?
Again I only ask that you hold my hand, for Lord, I can't take another fall!

When the darkness of the world appears at night draw me near as the day pass.

The sun becomes the moon giving me the strength to make it home; Lord guide my feet for at times my shoes are too small and look into my heart

As I can't fight this war alone and for all those who would once walk beside me that have all passed on

A. L. WATKINES

PRECIOUS
LORD

Look into my heart and tell me what it that you see within me
Help me to walk, do and be as you would have me to be
For in my walk there are those who don't understand the
man within me

So take my hand precious Lord
and lead me on as only you know me better
lead me on as you walk beside me
and help me to stand in case I might slip and fall

For Lord I am tired
At this time I am weak
But when I think of where you have brought me from
something moves inside of me

THE BEST OF BOTH WORLDS

COME AS YOU ARE

He stood there in the doorway with open hands. For he was a not a Godly looking man. Now upon his body could be seen the dirt of the land and there upon his hands were the signs of blood stains which were a sign of his hurt and pain. Yet within his eyes could be seen the ray of the sun.

From a distance the scent that seemed to project itself from his body would make the people around him turn and walk the other way.

The hair upon his head looked as if a comb had never touched it and that moss and other bugs had made their home within it. The color of his skin was that of an eclipse covering the sun and his breath smelt like whiskey and wine mixed or whatever he could get his hands upon to drink in his past. His voice was so powerful as if he was John the Baptize telling of Jesus coming. His faith was strong and as he stood in the doorway with open hands.

This not so Godly looking man stood saying "Come to me as you are" because he knew the word of God. If a person looked closely they could see the words 'Jesus Saves' tattooed upon his arms. Many people refused to take him seriously as a man of God.

Many saw him as a nut job standing in the doorway of an old abandoned church of long ago; saying with his arms opened "Come to me as you are". No one knew where he came from but for two weeks he stood in front of the church with his arms opened saying "Come to me as you are". Then one day he was gone and the following day the old abandoned church was destroyed.

TODAY I
GIVE YOU PEACE

Today I stood by the ocean and listened to the waves of the sea as I listened I could hear God's voice talking to me He said, "My son look at how I calm the waters of this sea, feed the fish and other critters with ease. Don't you know just like them I can give you the same peace and supply your needs?"

He then said "Son look at the birds, how they fly above you with their wings, look at the tree that is planted in the middle of the sea – growing leaves. Don't you know by now just like them, I can give you the power to multiply and spread forth your leaves if you just keep the faith and believe in me."

He then said, "Feel the air here. It's blowing between the buildings with peace. Don't you know I can do the same for you if you will just open your Bible and read because I am the King of Kings, the Sun and the Moon. I created all these things and for that reason I give you peace today!"

IN THE LORD'S PRESENCE

Today I was in the presence of the Lord and he jumped started my heart. For today unlike any other day He saw something within me and once again He granted me the gift of life. Not only did He wake me up this morning out of my sleep; He allowed me to walk into my kitchen to find food there to eat. I looked in my closet and there were clothes to place upon my body. I looked into my bathroom mirror and I saw that He had placed me upon another level. He opened my ears that I might hear Him speak to me and He touched my eyes that I might see people as He see them to be.

He gave me wisdom to share with others as He has shared His wisdom with me. He gave me knowledge unlike any knowledge I have ever received. Before I knew it He touched me and something new came over me like the water running down an ocean cleansing my soul to the point I know that He already lives down inside of me. For blessed is the man that possess rightness, so today I am blessed and highly favored in the presence of the Lord.

For today I am in the presence of the Lord. Today I had a promise from the Lord. He told me that I could laugh at my enemies. I owe Him praises; for I waiver not at the promises of the Lord through unbelief for what God promises. He is able to perform it. Yes today I am in the presence of the Lord and I saw the sun shine before me. I heard a bird sing a special song just for me. I felt the presence of my mother and grandmother watching over me and I felt the spirit of those who have prayed for me. For today is a good day all because I am in the presence of the Lord; He has helped me to be the man I needed to be all the while helping me to understand there is a testimony within me.

A. L. WATKINES

ACKNOWLEDGMENT

First and foremost, I thank the Almighty God, who have seen things in me that no other man or woman have seen. I thank Him for allowing me to emanate for the family in which I was raised and who shared my worldly views. It was these views that were shaped by all the other people I have gotten to know as well all the spiritual elements and graphic boundaries I have survived in this long arduous Christen walk.

Secondly, I would especially like to thank my mother, whose undying love for her children drove us to seek a higher education as well as a higher walk with God. She refused to allow us to be cheated or cast in a group.

I want to thank the late Pastor William Eaton of New Faith Church of God in Christ for giving me the power to minister the word of God every 4th Friday night in bible study.

I thank God for all the people I have encountered in my daily life who were an asset, confidant, friend or maybe a joy. Then there were the back biters even the haters who were envious of my God given gift. The lessons I have learned have been very hard and painful from both groups.

Made in the USA
Charleston, SC
13 March 2014